RECIPES

FROM A

Normal

Mum

RECIPES

FROM A

Normal Mum

HOLLY BELL

Photography by DAVID LOFTUS

Quadrille
PUBLISHING

For my children

Editorial director Jane O'Shea
Creative director Helen Lewis
Editor Louise McKeever
Designer Arielle Gamble
Photographer David Loftus
Props stylist Jo Harris
Production Aysun Hughes, Vincent Smith

First published in 2014 by
Quadrille Publishing Limited
Alhambra House
27–31 Charing Cross Road
London WC2H 0LS
www.quadrille.co.uk

Cataloguing in Publication Data: a catalogue record for this book is available from the
British Library.

ISBN 978 1 84949 419 9

Printed in China

NOTES
All spoon measures are level unless otherwise stated:
1 tsp = 5ml spoon; 1 tbsp = 15ml spoon.
If using the zest of citrus fruit, buy unwaxed fruit.
Timings are based on conventional ovens. If you are using a fan-assisted oven,
set your oven temperature approximately 10–15°C (1 gas mark) lower.
I use an electric oven and a gas hob.

CONTENTS

TIMES HAVE CHANGED

Everyone is strapped for cash. A few years ago it was common to suggest that the key to feeding a family well was spending a lot on core ingredients and then doing little to them, but now that advice feels out of touch. There's a pride in our revived make-do-and-mend gumption. You like my dress? Reduced to £10. This soup? 10p a portion. Saving money is savvy. Shopping well is savvy. Using a book with killer recipes that makes food taste amazing for a good price (not cheaply; I don't profess to be an economy gastronomy expert) is the ultimate in savvy.

We're going back to the age of my grandmother's youth where women (and men) took averagely priced ingredients and did ingenious things with them to make them taste wonderful. That is what this book and my blog are all about. And they don't rely on offal to do it. I started my blog over three years ago because I read yet another ridiculous recipe in a national newspaper. I'm a stay-at-home mum with two little boys and am fed up with reading recipes that involve a specialised shopping trip and an outlay of at least £30 – while professing to be a weeknight supper for regular people. I just don't believe that this is how families feed themselves. So I started to document what I cook for and with my family, and for my beloved friends, through a blog: www.recipesfromanormalmum.com. Recipes from me, a normal mum, for other normal mums and dads. And what is normal? Well it was supposed to be poking fun at the way I and so many mums describe ourselves. Does anyone know? Whatever it is, there's no denying the blog has struck a chord with readers from all over the world.

I try to make sure that the recipes are economical, tasty and the kind of dish that's requested again. If the core ingredients do cost that bit more then they're for recipes that produce leftovers or feed a crowd. I get inspiration from everywhere – they spring from memories of flavours from my youth, family favourites and even dreams (don't laugh!). But mostly they come from trial and error, testing them on my taste team, consisting of an almost forty-year-old man who thinks a meal without meat is a form of abuse, a five-year-old with a varied palate and a three-year-old with strong opinions that change often. And this is all done with not much time and a modest budget.

You'll find a few recipes that are on the blog purely because they're so popular it seemed foolish to leave them out. But there are also lots of new recipes which provide inventive, economical and simple answers to the question 'what can I give them?'. I've divided my recipes into chapters that reflect the varied themes and occasions in our lives. We are all pulled in so many directions, myself as a wife, a mother, a daughter, a friend, a writer… that we need a go-to recipe book that truly is a helping hand. Whether it is baking for your children's parties, economical recipes for when faced with feeding a very large, hungry crowd, or speedy grown-up weeknight suppers, as well as ideas for when you need to feed little people quickly, this is a book you can turn to no matter what aspect of family life you're approaching that day.

DOING IT YOUR WAY

It took me a few years of motherhood to find my feet in terms of how our family conducts itself. Some of the things I did and allowed in the early days make me blush now. We all have to find our way as parents and negotiate what's acceptable, what isn't, where we go the extra mile and where we take shortcuts. A big part of that is feeding. We're all obsessed with what goes into our offsprings' bodies. Nurturing is food.

Obvious though it is, it's worth reasserting that all children are different and so too are all parents. When it comes to feeding I think it's useful to draw a marker between savvy and worthy – decide where your line lies. I don't grow my own veg, but you will find me baking my own bread and making edible presents to save a few pennies.

I also try not to let stress infringe too much on meal times. The chat is kept light, the food is often familiar and as long as they try new things now and again I'm happy. Sometimes they spill drinks, and sometimes they don't like things that only yesterday they adored. This will pass. And there's a bonus to serving up familiar food. It creates rituals and routine that will ultimately be passed on to their own children.

A FEW OF MY FAVOURITE THINGS

I don't have a big kitchen so every single item has to earn its right to stay.

Freezer: I love my freezer; it's my main store cupboard. It houses caramelised onions in ice cube trays, Parmesan rinds to chuck into soup, breadcrumbs, red berries, scones, soup, stock, bread rolls, milk, butter, grated cheddar cheese, peas, prawns...

Food processor: My processor is large but it saves me having to chop and grate. I've managed to buy one for under £35 in the past.

Handheld stick blender: I think my love for this lies in how easy it is to clean. I mainly use it for soups, pastes and making purées for babies.

Microwave: I'm not a fan of ready meals but for zapping leftovers, giving jacket potatoes a head start and conjuring speedy cakey puddings, there is no other way.

Digital scales: My baking improved hugely when I invested in a set of digital scales. This is obvious but don't forget to reset back to 0 before you add each new ingredient.

Slow cooker: I love mine, but only once I accepted its limitations. Slow cookers don't so much save you time – you still need to fry the ingredients and brown the meat, but they do cook whilst you're out all day and they cost less to run than the oven.

Non-stick frying pan: Mine cost just £5 and I find I need less fat when using it.

Sandwich toaster: Last year my husband bought me a deep-fill sandwich toaster for Christmas and for me it was up there with diamonds. I love toasties in all their guises.

Sharp knives: It's obvious but I've lost count of how many times I've soldiered on with a blunt knife. Accidents happen more with blunt knives as they slip and slide across food.

Sharp scissors: I use scissors more than most in the kitchen. I use them for snipping off pieces of pizza dough, to cut bacon sandwiches and to chop herbs into a dish.

Soup ladle: Makes for less mess and less cleaning, and that makes me happy.

Silicone spatula: This scrapes absolutely all of the batter out of the bowl.

Microplane grater: These are super sharp and make short work of hard cheese, garlic, ginger, nutmeg and zest. Easy to clean too.

Dough scraper: Order these online – plastic ones are about 50p and are better than metal as there's less chance of scratching your work surface.

Oven thermometer: If you consistently find recipes fail then try an oven thermometer, as you may be surprised at your oven's interpretation of 180°C.

Cooling racks: These help baked goods cool without getting soggy bottoms. You really need to have two. Delicate sponge will stick to a cooling rack when warm, ripping the top off as you peel them, so line with greaseproof paper first.

Good greaseproof paper: I love the white greaseproof paper that genuinely does not stick and it also doubles up as excellent tracing paper.

Disposable, easygrip icing bags: A roll of these lasts me a long time. Annoyingly, fabric ones often seep icing. Wash the disposable ones really well for another use. As for nozzles, I only use a star tip, a Wilton 1M.

Cake lifter: This little gem was introduced to me by *The Great British Bake Off* team. It's a huge flat paddle used to lift cakes from their spring-bottomed bases or to prise tarts and quiches from theirs without them breaking or spilling their contents.

Tea strainer: The type that clamps together like little jaws. Use it to dredge loaves in flour pre baking, tap icing sugar over cakes and pastries and pour boiling water over fresh mint and ginger for a refreshing tisane.

Stand mixer: I love my KitchenAid stand mixer. These are not essential and certainly a considered purchase but they do make life simpler. I look at kitchen purchases the same way I do clothes; cost per use. So despite costing £300 I already have the mixer down to 50p per use. And that cost will only reduce as the years pass.

A no-muscles-required corkscrew: Goes without saying doesn't it? Cheers!

Being an only child meant I was obsessed with large families. I loved the idea of their natural camaraderie and sitting shoulder to shoulder at the dinner table. Of course the queueing for the bathroom, squabbling over toys, complete lack of privacy and the incessant din that goes with having a large brood was lost on me. All I saw was the communal eating of heavily laden platters and, being a greedy child, I was sold. I planned a large family and an even larger table.

It turns out I have neither the pain threshold nor the wallet for a very large family, but I was right about enjoying huge family gatherings. I'm never happier than when the grandparents, aunties, uncles, cousins and friends descend. Feeding a crowd of varying age can be the most difficult brief, for no one really wants to make different meals do they? What's needed are one-size-fits-all recipes that will keep everyone happy.

As much as I love preparing food for people I love, I want to enjoy it too. No one likes a martyr, in fact there's nothing that'll put folks off their food more than the chef sweating in the kitchen, refraining from joining in. The secret to any good gathering is, I think, to care lots and lots about the event right up until the moment the doorbell rings and then to simply set about, as the host, having the best time possible. You set the fun-o-meter, so don't be a stick in the kitchen.

The More the Merrier

My seven-hour honey and rosemary lamb

The common advice about having a crowd over for dinner is to never attempt a recipe you're unfamiliar with. I disagree. When else do you have the opportunity to make something different? Family and friends are the perfect audience to try new ideas out on. Especially when you can put it in the oven hours before dinnertime. And this recipe is liked by all. You can use a larger leg of lamb if you need to feed more people — just make sure it will fit in your roasting tray!

Serves 4–6

3 carrots, peeled and sliced
  in half lengthways
5 onions, peeled and sliced
  in half
2 tbsp vegetable or
  groundnut oil
1 leg of lamb (about 2kg)
2 sprigs of rosemary, leaves
  finely chopped or 2 tbsp
  dried rosemary
2 tbsp thick honey
1 tsp salt
2 tsp ground black pepper
250ml white wine
300ml warm lamb or vegetable
  stock (a stock cube is fine)

Preheat the oven to 120°C/gas mark ½. Find a large roasting tin that will fit your lamb and line with a very long length of foil (I keep a roll of mammoth extra strong foil just for this dish — it needs to be big enough to wrap around the tin a couple of times). Place the carrots and onions in the bottom of the tin to form a trivet (a vegetable resting place if you will).

Heat the oil in a large frying pan and brown the lamb on as many sides as you can get into contact with the heat. I wrap my hands in a clean tea towel and manoeuvre the lamb, rather than using any tongues. You can skip this but the lamb will not brown in the oven and will emerge an unappetising shade of beige.

Place the lamb on top of the trivet. Mix the rosemary leaves with the honey, salt and pepper and rub all over the top side of the lamb. Pour the wine and stock into the bottom of the tin. Wrap the whole tin in foil, until it's completely sealed — this bit is very important as if there's any way for the heat to escape your lamb won't be cooked when you come to unwrap it. I roll the foil over many times at each join. Or use a casserole dish with a lid.

Forget about it in the oven for 7 hours, then break the foil open at the table and carve with spoons for maximum excitement. Serve with crunchy slaw and clean tasting steamed rice in the summer or nutmeg braised leeks and dauphinoise potatoes in the winter: place 1kg of waxy potatoes like Desiree, peeled, very thinly sliced and well seasoned in a ceramic dish and cover with double cream. Add a crushed garlic clove and bake at 190°C/gas mark 5 for about 40 minutes or until tender.

Greek-inspired meatballs

Being an easy blusher, I like to think I notice embarrassment at ten paces. And when it comes to food, we apologise far too much for what we use and produce in our kitchens, especially when it comes to seasoning. Dried herbs are almost a dirty secret. Well, no longer! We need to reclaim dried herbs and stop being so sniffy. After all, the Italians and the Greeks have been using them without so much as a sorry or a stutter for many years. Long live dried herbs; they save us money and, used right, taste great. Here's a recipe using dried oregano. Don't even think about using the fresh stuff.

Serves 6 (or 4 with leftovers to fight over)

1 tbsp olive oil
500g lamb mince
75g fresh breadcrumbs
30ml whole milk
1 large egg
1 tsp salt
1 tsp ground black pepper
1 tsp dried oregano
60g feta cheese, crumbled

Grease a large roasting tray with the oil and preheat the oven to 180°C/gas mark 4. In a large bowl, mix together the mince, breadcrumbs, milk, egg, salt, pepper and oregano. Use your hands to make sure every ingredient is really well distributed. You can use a food processor to do this but beware of over mixing it into sludge. Add the crumbled feta and mix through gently with your hands.

Dip your hands in some cold water and form meatballs from the mixture, each about the size of a golf ball. I try to get the kids involved in this job if I can; many hands make light work and all that. Place each meatball on the greased tray and continue until the entire mixture has been used. Bake for 35 minutes, turning after 20 minutes. I serve these with either a simple feta-less Greek salad, my quick tomato sauce (from pizza parties, see page 182) with orzo pasta or just toasted pitta with tzatziki. They're great cold in lunchboxes the next day too.

Ideas for feta cheese

Bake cubes in the oven until brown and serve with a spoonful of honey and fresh figs or chilled sliced apple. Or crumble and mix into soured cream with chopped spring onion and grated cucumber for a light dip. Or slice and mix with watermelon chunks, olives and balsamic vinegar for a speedy, fresh salad. Or marinate cubes in a jar filled with olive oil, dried oregano, sliced garlic and black olives, to keep in the fridge to nibble on for the next fortnight.

Mysteriously meaty veggie chickpea burgers

Not mysterious in a 'Surprise! We contain liver!' way, as I really don't suppose vegetarians would be very impressed by that! These are mysterious as, despite containing zero meat, they fill you up so much you can't help feeling you've eaten a lot of protein; which of course you have, only in pulse format.

The men in my life (save my eldest son) search their plates for meat products. However, these burgers satisfy their Neanderthal palates and keep my almost vegetarian son happy. They're a thrifty dish too, so they are perfect for larger gatherings.

Makes 10 burgers and serves 10 with buns, chips and salad or 5 without

2 small onions, peeled and
   finely chopped
1 tsp ground cumin
1 tsp ground coriander
1 tbsp groundnut or sunflower
   oil, plus a little extra
   for frying
2 x 400g tins of chickpeas,
   drained and rinsed
4 garlic cloves, peeled
   and crushed
1 large egg
80g breadcrumbs (crumble up
   stale bread or whizz lightly
   toasted bread in a food
   processor)
100g carrots (about 2 large),
   peeled and finely grated

Preheat the oven to 180°C/gas mark 4. In a pan over a low heat, fry the onions, cumin and coriander in the oil until soft and starting to brown at the edges. Remove from the heat and let cool a little. Blend all the other ingredients except the carrot to a paste using a food processor or stick blender. Stir in the onions and carrot. Shape the mixture into 10 burgers using wet hands and chill for 10 minutes.

In batches, fry the burgers in the onion pan with a little extra oil for 3 minutes or until lightly browned. Turn over carefully with a fish slice and repeat until the other side is browned. Keep warm in the oven until all the burgers are cooked and serve with toasted buns, chips (see page 44) and lots of salad.

If you have any left over keep them in the fridge and take to work in lunchboxes the next day with lots of salad and a pitta bread. These are also delicious made into tiny fried patties and served with drinks when you are having friends over.

French bread monster toastie

The key with this one is to know your audience. You can't make this for a gathering where your brother or sister are bringing their new belle or beau, you need to know your guests' foodie foibles and be sure everyone will like the filling. For this is easy one-size-fits-all fayre; an elasticated trouser of a recipe.

Serves 6–8

1 French stick

Filling of your choice:

The Man-wich: Steak, fried onions, mushrooms and cheddar (pictured)

The Amended Reuben: Pastrami, mustard, pickles and rocket

The Wanda: Gruyère, tuna, capers and pea shoots

The Italian Job: Mozzarella, basil and Parma ham

Best of British: Sliced roast beef, horseradish, radish and watercress

All the Colours Veggie: Crumbled goat's cheese, beetroot, tinned and drained artichokes, mayonnaise, wholegrain mustard and salad leaves

The Hash and Tangle: Corned beef, slices of cooked new potatoes, fried onions and HP sauce

The Chicken Satay Sway: Sliced leftover roast chicken, grated carrot, fresh coriander and sweet chilli sauce mixed with a little peanut butter

The [insert surname] Special: Your call!

Cut the French stick in half lengthways. This needs to be able to fit under your grill, so cut accordingly. Toast the bread under a hot grill and then layer the filling on one side of the bread and place the lid back on. If your filling has cheese in it, I'd crumble or grate it onto both open sides of the bread before grilling as melted cheese always adds to a sandwich, I think.

Serve whole on a large platter with a serrated knife to hand so that people can portion up the toastie themselves. Minimum effort, maximum taste. If you're feeling a little more energetic you might want to serve with the orzo salad on page 112 or chargrilled carrot salad on page 96 but don't feel you have to.

Tapenade black breast roast chicken

Roast chicken isn't hard to get right. A touch of oil, maybe a little massage of butter, an onion and a lemon and into a hot oven and hey presto, lunch is served. Introducing other flavours can feel a bit like gilding the lily. Thai roast chicken is not for me. Yet this tapenade stuffing adds a saltiness to the chicken that feels just right. I don't use anchovies, they're just too much for a dainty bird. But the basil adds a Provençal feel.

Serves 6 with side dishes

1 large chicken
50ml olive oil
90g pitted black olives
28g pack of basil leaves, washed
2 tbsp capers, drained
2 garlic cloves, crushed
Finely grated zest and juice of 1 lemon
1 tsp Dijon mustard

Ideas for capers

Fry white fish fillets in a little foaming butter with a couple of teaspoons of capers and serve with lots of steamed sugar snap peas and a little bread for mopping up the juices. Or include capers and kale in homemade pesto for extra tang and an iron hit. Or if you're not an anchovy fan, a niçoise salad is lifted by a few capers, a perfect substitution for their saltiness.

Wash the chicken in cold water then pat dry with kitchen roll. Place in a roasting tray breast side up.

Make the tapenade by blending together the oil, olives, basil, capers, garlic, lemon zest and juice and mustard in a food processor or using a stick blender. Whizz until well blended but leaving some texture – you need to see that there are little pieces of olives in it. Keep the remains of the lemon and stuff it into the chicken cavity.

Preheat the oven to 200°C/gas mark 6. Use a pair of scissors to cut two holes in the skin at the top end of the bird. This is the narrow end at the top of the breasts. Using your fingers, gently ease the skin apart from the breast meat, creating pockets between the skin and the meat. Carefully spoon the tapenade into the pockets, massaging the stuffing down so that it covers the whole breast. This will ensure that the flavours permeate all of the meat from the breast downwards.

Calculate the bird's cooking time; you will need to roast it for 25 minutes per 500g plus an extra 25 minutes. Place in the oven and cook for the specified time. The bird is ready when the juices run clear when the thickest part of the thigh is pierced. Please don't despair if the breast bursts in the oven; this happens very occasionally and whilst it looks a little horror film-esque, the flavour is in no way compromised, and oddly the stuffing seems to stay put. I serve this with ratatouille and a few rosemary roasted potatoes for good measure.

Stew's keema matar

This isn't my recipe, it's my husband's. It's probably one of my favourite dinners, especially when there are lots of mouths to feed. The lamb is fatty and satiating so a little goes a long way. I can't decide whether I prefer it with a side of fluffy white basmati rice or wrapped in flatbreads and eaten street-food style by hand. My advice is to try both.

Serves 4–6 depending on appetites

1 tbsp groundnut or
   sunflower oil
2 onions, peeled and
   finely chopped
1½ tsp coriander seeds
1 tsp cumin seeds
1 tsp dried chilli flakes
6 garlic cloves, peeled
   and crushed
600g lamb mince
1 thumbnail-sized piece
   of fresh ginger, peeled
   and grated
2 medium heat red chillies,
   finely chopped
400g tin of chopped tomatoes
200g frozen petit pois
1 tsp garam masala (bought or
   homemade, see page 219)

Heat the oil in a frying pan over a medium heat until hot, then add the onions and fry until golden-brown, stirring occasionally. Meanwhile heat a small non-stick pan and fry the coriander and cumin seeds in the dry, hot pan until aromatic – take care not to let them burn. Transfer the spices to a pestle and mortar, add the chilli flakes and grind to a fine powder. You can miss the stage of dry frying and simply grind the spices if you don't have the time or inclination but it does add a wonderful depth of flavour. Set the spices aside for later.

Add the garlic, lamb, ginger, fresh chillies and ground spices to the fried onions and stir. Turn the heat down and add the chopped tomatoes. Refill the tomato tin with cold water and add to the pan. Simmer for 30 minutes. Just before serving stir through the peas and the garam masala and leave to warm through for 5 minutes or until the peas are cooked.

Serve with fluffy basmati rice or flatbreads and raita. Leftovers are a blessing with this dish. This curry tastes better the next day simply reheated, or if you fancy something a bit different, use the mixture as a spicy shepherd's pie base: simply add mashed potato to the top and bake at 180°C/gas mark 4 for 40 minutes.

Caponata tart

This is a great alternative to quiche. It can be eaten cold, assembled last minute and doesn't have the cold eggy clagginess of a day-old quiche. It feels like it should be eaten amongst olive groves with a glass of something very cold and Italian. In reality it works equally well for lunch with a cup of tea. If possible make the caponata the day before you need it to allow the flavours to develop in the fridge.

Serves 8–10

For the pastry and filling:

280g plain flour
1 tsp paprika
140g very cold butter,
    cut into 1cm cubes
75–80ml very cold water
250g cream cheese
Handful of flat-leaf
    parsley leaves

For the caponata:

4 tbsp olive oil
2 large onions, peeled
    and cut into 2cm pieces
3 celery stalks, cut into
    2cm chunks
1 red pepper, deseeded
    and cut into 2cm chunks
2 aubergines (about 500g in
    total), stalks removed and
    cut into 2cm chunks
2 tbsp capers, drained
20 pitted green olives
15g sugar
1 tbsp red wine vinegar
2 tbsp tomato purée
1 tsp salt
Ground black pepper,
    to taste

Make the pastry. Mix the flour and paprika. Stir the butter into the flour using a blunt knife, until all the pieces are well coated. Wash your hands in cold water and rub the butter into the flour until you have a very fine breadcrumb-like consistency. Using the blunt knife to mix, add enough icy water to just pull the pastry together. The humidity of the room and the type of flour will affect the amount of water needed, so just use enough to pull it together but not so much that it's sticky. Wrap in cling film and chill for 20 minutes.

Meanwhile, make the caponata. Heat the oil in a large frying pan and fry the onions, celery and pepper over a very low heat for 30 minutes until softened and cooked through. Tip into a large saucepan. Fry batches of the aubergine in the empty dry frying pan for 5 minutes until browned, and add to the saucepan. Add all of the remaining caponata ingredients with 3 table-spoons of water to the saucepan and simmer on a low heat for 25 minutes until very tender and cooked, but with the vegetables retaining their shape. Remove from the heat and set aside.

Preheat the oven to 200°C/gas mark 6. Roll the pastry out on a floured surface into a circle about 30cm across and the thickness of a pound coin. Put both hands under the pastry, palms facing up and fingers spread wide, and gently transfer to a 22cm loose-bottomed tart tin. Gently push the pastry into the corners and run the rolling pin over the top to trim the pastry. Cover with greaseproof paper and fill with baking beans, uncooked rice or pulses (this will stop the pastry from puffing up as it cooks) and bake blind for 20 minutes. Remove the beans and paper and bake for another 5–10 minutes until completely baked through. Remove from the oven and leave to cool completely, still in the tin, on a wire rack.

To assemble, remove the case from the tin and place on a plate. Spread the cream cheese onto the base using the back of a spoon. Using a slotted spoon to drain away any excess moisture, spoon the still warm caponata on top, making a mountain of vegetables. Scatter over the parsley and serve immediately, or cold the next day with barbecued meats or green salad. Or both.

Triple S lasagne

Rhubarb and custard, cheese and red wine, chilli and chocolate… Some flavours
are just meant to be together, they never fight for attention. And the triple whammy
of sausages, squash and sage is a beautiful thing. The squash provides extra meatiness
through texture and the sage brings the béchamel sauce front and centre so that
overall, the sausage doesn't steal the show, as it often does. Make this in stages by
grilling the sausages and roasting the vegetables the day before.

Serves 6

12 large, good-quality sausages
½ butternut squash (about
    650g), peeled, deseeded and
    chopped into 3cm chunks
2 large onions, peeled and
    chopped to 2cm pieces
2 tbsp olive oil
400g tin of chopped tomatoes
100g butter
3 sage leaves, finely chopped
100g plain flour
Ground black pepper, to taste
645ml whole or semi-
    skimmed milk
9 lasagne sheets
50g Parmesan, finely grated

Ideas for fresh sage

Use a few leaves along with
a lemon to stuff a chicken
for an aromatic roast. Or fry
leaves in butter and serve
over cooked pasta with
grated cheese for a quick
supper. Or just one leaf,
finely chopped and added to
the cheese biscuits (see page
161) morphs these morsels
into a post-dinner offering.

Grill the sausages until browned and cooked through on all
sides; this takes about 15 minutes. Leave them to cool then
slice lengthways into three long strips.

Meanwhile, preheat the oven to 200°C/gas mark 6. Put the
squash and onion into a roasting tin measuring 26 x 20cm,
7cm deep and drizzle with oil. Roast in the oven for 30 minutes
until cooked through and browned, then add the tomatoes and
roast for another 15 minutes. Remove from the oven and set
aside to cool a little before mashing a little to break up the squash
pieces. Don't be too thorough though as you don't want a purée.

Make the béchamel by melting the butter with the sage leaves
in a saucepan over a medium heat. Add the flour and pepper and
whisk until a smooth paste forms. Cook off the flour for 1 minute
then turn the heat to low, add a little milk and whisk well. Add
some more before whisking again and so on, until all the milk is
added and the sauce is thick and smooth. Remove from the heat.

Assemble the lasagne by placing half the sausage slices in
the bottom of the roasting tray, covering with half of the squash
sauce. Add a layer of lasagne (3 sheets) and then half the
béchamel sauce. Cover with another layer of lasagne, followed
by the rest of the sausages and the remainder of the squash.
Lay over the final sheets of lasagne and cover completely with
the remaining béchamel. Sprinkle with Parmesan and bake for
35–45 minutes or until a knife slips through the pasta easily.
Serve with a green salad.

Banoffee hazelnut cookie crumble

Hands up. I will try and shoe-horn bananas, toffee and cream into almost anything.
I even found myself making mini banoffee pavlovas – as if meringue needed extra
sweetness! (It does; try it.) Crumbles can be a disappointment, a hiding place for
unloved fruit past its best. This however is no place for hide and seek. It's loved by all.

Make your own caramel by all means. It's easy enough, just heat 210g caster sugar
in a large saucepan until brown and dissolved and add 80g butter. Let the butter
melt and then take off the heat. Whisk in 110ml double cream and you are done!
But I don't really like melting sugar and that's nothing to be ashamed of.

Serves 6-8

4 large bananas, sliced
  in half lengthways
397g tin of caramel
125g toasted hazelnuts, finely
  chopped (I buy them already
  toasted but you can gently
  toast them in a hot oven
  and chop once cool)
225g plain flour
90g granulated brown sugar
½ tsp baking powder
170g butter, melted

Preheat the oven to 180°C/gas mark 4. Lay the bananas out in
a single layer in an ovenproof dish about 26 x 18cm, 6cm deep.
Give the tin of caramel a good stir to loosen it and spoon over
the bananas evenly.

Mix together the nuts, flour, sugar and baking powder in a large
bowl. Stir the butter through the dry mixture until it begins to
gather into clumps. Spoon the crumble over the bananas and
caramel and bake for 35–40 minutes until the top is bubbling
and brown. Serve with ice cream and a large glass of milk.

If there are any leftovers, which I doubt, roughly mix with vanilla
ice cream to make banoffee cookie crumble ice cream.

Ideas for hazelnuts

Add to the biscotti (page 214) or brownies (page 143) mixture
for a nutty hit. Or mix with breadcrumbs, rosemary, thyme and
a little egg to make a stuffing to accompany roast pork. Or add
to a pan of milk, bring to the boil, turn down to barely a simmer
and steep for 30 minutes before using the milk in coffee and hot
chocolate, for a coffee shop syrup-style nut delivery without any
of the sugar.

Chocolate orange trifle

I once had a boyfriend called Robin. Our relationship was doomed to failure as, apart from the prospect of spending my life as one half of a comedy Christmas couple, we argued about everything except this pudding. Robin's mother introduced me to this one Christmas. Eat, undo the top button of your jeans and sit back. You can use fresh oranges instead of the tinned clementines but I think they ruin the texture.

Serves 12

For the cake:

60g self-raising flour
60g salted butter, softened
85g caster sugar
1 large egg, at room
    temperature
1 tbsp whole or semi-
    skimmed milk
¼ tsp baking powder
1 orange
50ml Cointreau™

Or

250g plain vanilla sponge cake

For the rest of the assembly:

600ml double cream
2 x 135g packs orange jelly;
    I use Hartley's (this will leave
    you with some excess jelly)
2 x 312g tins of clementines,
    drained weight 175g
465g chocolate custard
12 chocolate orange segments
    or curls of orange chocolate

You need a 2.2 litre trifle bowl. Or make individual portions in smaller bowls if sharing is difficult.

If you are making this for a large gathering you may already feel stressed. Far be it for me to add to this, so if the thought of making the sponge makes you groan then buy a cake and be done with it.

If making the sponge, pop 5 muffin cases into a 12-hole muffin tin and preheat the oven to 170°C/gas mark 3. Beat the flour, butter, 60g of the sugar, egg, milk and baking powder until pale and creamy, about 4 minutes with a mixer or 8 minutes with a wooden spoon. Finely grate the zest of the orange and add half to the batter and half to the double cream for later. Stir the batter to combine. Spoon into the cases and bake for 15–20 minutes until well risen, lightly browned and a skewer comes out clean.

As soon as the cakes are out of the oven (or packet), heat the remaining 25g of sugar and the Cointreau™ on the hob until the sugar dissolves. Poke holes all over the cakes using a skewer and pour the syrup over the top. Leave to cool on a wire rack.

Make the jelly according to the packet instructions, replacing a little water with the juice from the zested orange. This makes 1.14 litres. Leave in the fridge until almost set.

Remove the cake cases, slice into pieces and line the bottom of the dish. Scatter over the clementines, then top with about 800ml of the jelly. Leave the rest of the jelly in a bowl for eating later.

Pour over the custard and level it using the back of a spoon. Using an electric or handheld whisk, whip the cream with the added zest to medium peaks and spoon over the top. Decorate with chocolate orange segments or curls and dig in.

Ginger, mango, pear & papaya ripple ice cream

Ice cream is the perfect low-stress pudding when there's a crowd to cater for. It is almost universally appealing and can be happily ensconced in the freezer from the day before.

As a child, ice cream was exotic if it sported an unusual fruit; I will never forget the joy of licking blackcurrant ice cream in the summer of '88 at the local museum. Of late, ice cream just isn't ice cream if it doesn't have a pudding stirred in. Crème brûlée, tiramisu... Well here's a gentle ice cream — simple fruit purée and a ginger kick. Ginger may seem like an adult flavour, but children seem to love it. Admittedly, this isn't the cheapest ice cream to make, but the result is worth spending that little bit extra for.

Makes 1 litre

600ml double cream
397g tin of condensed milk
8 pieces of crystallised ginger, finely chopped
2 x 60g sachets of mango, pear and papaya purée

In a large mixing bowl, whisk together the cream and the condensed milk until the mixture leaves ribbony trails when the whisk is lifted out of the mixture. Pour into a 1 litre plastic container, scatter the ginger pieces over the creamy mixture and stir through gently. Lastly, lightly stir through the purée, though not fully, to create a ripple effect. Freeze for at least 4 hours or preferably overnight.

Remove from the freezer 20 minutes before serving. Serve alone or with slices of mango.

Ideas for crystallised ginger

Dip in dark chocolate and leave to solidify for an after-dinner nibble. Or make 18 low sugar muesli ginger biscuits that are great for breakfast on the run: mix 100g melted butter, 2 large eggs, 100g plain flour, 360g muesli and 60g chopped crystallised ginger, drop heaped tablespoons of the mixture onto a lined baking sheet and bake at 180°C/gas mark 4 for 10–15 minutes.

Chocolate chip lime meringue pie

This was inspired by the sugary sweet chocolate limes my friends and I used to buy on the way to school (school bus arrival allowing). You can make the pastry and curd the day before you need them — simply keep the pastry case in a tin and the curd covered in the fridge. If making curd feels a bit too much like hard work then replace with the bought variety and don't apologise for it.

Serves 12

For the pastry:
140g cold salted butter, cut into 1cm cubes
280g plain flour, plus extra for dusting
100g plain chocolate chips (the baking ones, not chopped up chocolate)
1 large egg, beaten

For the curd:
4 egg yolks, beaten
200g caster sugar
1 tbsp plain flour
25g cornflour
Finely grated zest and juice of 3 limes
30g butter
A little green food colouring (optional)

For the meringue:
4 egg whites
125g caster sugar

Preheat the oven to 180°C/gas mark 4. Make the pastry by rubbing the butter into the flour until you have a breadcrumb-like consistency. Stir through the chocolate chips and then use a blunt knife to mix in the egg to bind the mixture. Wrap in cling film and chill for 20 minutes.

Roll the pastry out on a floured work surface to a rough circle about 30cm across and the thickness of a pound coin. Place both hands under the pastry, palms up and fingers spread wide and transfer to a 26cm loose-bottomed tart tin. This pastry is prone to cracking as you move it because of the chocolate; just move it and patch and mend the rips and edges once in the tin. There will be just enough pastry, with no leftovers.

Cover the pastry with greaseproof paper and fill with baking beans, dried rice or pulses and bake blind for 20 minutes. Remove the paper and beans and bake for another 10 minutes until completely cooked through and golden. Remove from the oven and leave to cool. Turn off the heat.

Meanwhile, make the curd. Place the yolks in a heatproof bowl and lightly whisk. Whisk the sugar, flour and cornflour in a pan over a medium heat. Stir in 350ml of water, lime zest and juice and continue to cook over a medium heat, whisking constantly until the mixture comes to the boil. Stir in the butter until dissolved and remove from the heat.

Add a third of the hot mixture to the yolks, whisking constantly. Pour this mixture back into the pan and return to the heat. Turn the heat up, bring to the boil and whisk constantly to stop any lumps from forming. When the curd is thick and bubbling remove from the heat and stir the food colouring through, if using. Leave the curd to cool before making the meringue.

Preheat the oven to 170°C/gas mark 3. Whisk the egg whites using a mixer or handheld whisk until soft peaks form. Add a tablespoon of sugar at a time, whisking for 20 seconds after each addition, until it is all incorporated and the meringue is bright white and glossy. Fill the cold tart case with the cold curd. Spoon the meringue first around the edges of the case and then pile what's left into the middle to completely cover the curd and create a seal. Bake for 25 minutes until golden.

Give a child a poor diet and it's simply more of the same they crave. Give them mainly home-cooked meals, served with lots of veg followed by fruit-based puddings and that is what they will crave. It doesn't have to be difficult and no one need be smug. There are still lots of foods my kids don't like, but for me the emphasis is that they try new things. Food isn't frightening.

In a perfect world we'd eat as a family every night, but for us, that just isn't possible. My husband works beyond the boys' dinnertime so we save eating as a family for the weekend. Weekdays are all about finding delicious solutions for teatime that don't leave me seeking out tonic water before 7pm. These are designed for small people, but they're not half bad for bigger people too.

PURÉES VERSUS BABY LED...
I don't want to enter the whole weaning versus purée debate. I did a combination of purées in ever increasingly lumpy textures and handheld bits and bobs, which helped each of my sons learn to feed themselves. It worked for us, but really, anything goes. You choose, the recipes here can be blended up or served as they are.

THE WHATEVER YOU'RE EATING WITHOUT SALT PURÉE
When I was weaning my first son I used to make batches of food just for him, often dedicating whole Sundays to the task. No such schoolgirl error with my second-born. I invested in baby stock cubes and made all the family food low or no salt, then whizzed it into increasingly larger pieces as he got older. Anything he liked I'd make a larger portion of and freeze in ice cube trays for quick meals. Easy, cheap, nourishing — what's not to like?

Feeding Goldilocks & Baby Bear Too

McCauliflower macaroni cheese

Maybe it's genetic – my sons like cauliflower cheese and nursery style macaroni cheese almost as much as my husband does. This combines both dishes and uses crème fraîche rather than a roux sauce for ease and speed, hence the homage through a fast food name. The pasta serves as the 'bite' and of course much needed energy hit, with the cauliflower adding vitamins, flavour and thickening the sauce. For weaning age children I serve this with wedges of mild cheese to chew/throw on the floor.

Serves 2 children, scale up as required

60g macaroni
60g cauliflower (about
   2 florets), chopped into
   2cm chunks
1 tsp groundnut or
   sunflower oil
10g butter
½ small onion (about 25g),
   peeled and finely chopped
70g cheddar, grated (as strong
   as your child likes)
40g half-fat crème fraîche
Ground black pepper (optional)

Cook the macaroni according to the packet instructions, and 4 minutes before the end of the cooking time add the cauliflower.

Meanwhile, heat the oil and butter in a large pan and fry the onion over a low heat, until just softened but not browned, about 4 minutes. Once the pasta and cauliflower are soft and cooked through, drain and set aside. Add the cheese and the crème fraîche to the pan of onions. Without turning the heat up, stir until all the cheese has melted. Add the drained pasta, cauliflower and a little black pepper to the sauce and stir until thoroughly coated. Serve either as it is or scattered with some chopped ham if you like.

Ideas for cauliflower

Roast in the oven with a little oil then blitz with stock, cooked potato and a sautéed leek for a creamy textured soup and serve with a sprinkling of very finely chopped roasted hazelnuts for a posh starter. Or use steamed cauliflower in place of potatoes in a Spanish omelette for a less heavy alternative. Or it is delicious in almost any curry; it retains flavour in the tightly wound heads.

Cook Islanders curry

I had the pleasure of completing a round-the-world whistle-stop trip when I was just 22. I had lots of wonderful times and memories but over 10 years on, what do I remember most? Riding a horse waist deep in the sea, the bright lights and alien cuisine of Hong Kong or watching a transvestite dance troupe in San Francisco? No, no and no. A banana curry in the Cook Islands. Like any normal person I was suspicious of a banana curry but my goodness it was wonderful. Here's my tribute.

Makes 4 toddler servings or many ice cubes

2 tbsp groundnut oil
½ medium onion, peeled and finely chopped
2 garlic cloves, peeled and crushed
2cm piece of fresh ginger, peeled and finely diced
1 tsp turmeric
1 tsp garam masala (bought or homemade, see page 219)
1 chicken breast (about 160g), cut into 1cm cubes (you can use boneless thigh meat if you prefer)
1 banana, sliced (you want one that is as green as possible)
60ml cold water
2 tbsp sultanas
15g desiccated coconut

Heat the oil in a frying pan over a very low heat and fry the onion for 10 minutes until soft and just beginning to colour. Add the garlic, ginger, turmeric and garam masala and fry for 1 minute, then add the chicken and gently fry for 5 minutes until sealed. Add the banana, water and sultanas and leave to bubble away for 15 minutes. Add the coconut and serve as it is for older children or blended/mashed up a little for younger ones.

This freezes well, although the bananas will be a little discoloured upon thawing. Just stir well and make sure everything's piping hot before serving.

Ideas for desiccated coconut

For a grown-up treat try the holiday hammock cake (page 115) with its boozy coconut icing. Or add a few tablespoons to the flapjacks (page 134). Or if you're in the mood for confectionery then coconut lime ice always produces a smile – mix 295g of coconut with 295g of icing sugar and the zest of 1 lime, then tip in a 405g tin of condensed milk, stir well, press into a lined tin, chill overnight and cut into squares to serve.

Fish mornay sauce ice cubes

If you're only going to make one purée for your babies then I'd recommend this one. It's a multi-tasker. You can serve it with mashed potato and mashed up peas or add to cooked pasta and veggies for a quick fishy pasta dish. My mother always used to make her epic fish pie with a layer of mashed up boiled eggs, so in homage to her I serve this with wedges of hard-boiled egg or strips of omelette.

Pour the milk into a saucepan and add the fish. Bring the pan up to a simmer over a moderate heat; this takes about 3 minutes. As soon as the fish is opaque remove it from the heat – this will only take another minute or so. Remove the fish with a slotted spoon and set aside. Pour the cooking milk into a jug. Melt the butter in the saucepan then add the flour and whisk until smooth and no lumps are left. Cook for 1 minute over a medium heat then add a little of the milk, whisking all the time to get rid of any lumps. Keep adding the milk a little at a time and whisk until you have a thick, smooth sauce. Remove from the heat and stir in the cheese, some pepper and the nutmeg. Add the fish and either serve as is to older children or blend to a purée for babies.

Makes about 20 ice cubes

150ml whole milk
2 small fillets of white skinless
    fish such as coley or pollack
    (about 85g), cut into 2cm
    chunks
20g butter
20g plain flour
25g cheddar, grated
Ground black pepper (optional)
A pinch of freshly ground
    nutmeg

A sweet & melting inauthentic lamb tagine

Little ones are big fans of savoury and sweet combinations and I for one am with them there. This tagine includes a lovely sweet hit from the caramelised onions and apricots. My sons weren't big on rice when very young so I served this with strips of flatbread or breadsticks. It also freezes very well. I use my slow cooker to save on energy bills but you can cook it in a tightly lidded casserole dish on your oven's lowest setting.

Mix all the spices together in a large bowl, add the lamb and toss to cover. In a large frying pan over a low heat, fry the onion in the oil and sugar until the onions start to catch at the edges and caramelise. Tip the onions into your slow cooker or casserole dish. Turn the heat up under the frying pan and fry the spice-covered meat for 5 minutes until browned all over. Tip the lamb in with the onions and also add the garlic, tomatoes, apricots and sultanas and cook in the slow cooker on low or in the oven at 140°C/gas mark 1 for 5 hours, until the lamb is soft and falling apart.

Serve with cous cous, rice, tortilla wraps or carrots for dipping. This is especially loved by babies in puréed form.

Makes 6 small servings

1 tsp paprika
1 tsp ground ginger
1 tsp turmeric
1 tsp ground cinnamon
¼ tsp ground black pepper
200g lamb shoulder,
  cut into 3cm chunks
1 small onion, peeled
  and finely chopped
2 tbsp groundnut or
  sunflower oil
1 tbsp caster sugar
2 garlic cloves, peeled
  and crushed
400g tin of chopped tomatoes
40g dried apricots, quartered
30g sultanas

Ideas for dried apricots

Add 80g of chopped dried apricots and 1 tsp dried tarragon to scones (page 140) for an unexpected flavour combination. Or steep in fresh orange juice and 1 tablespoon of honey overnight and add to Greek yoghurt and granola in the morning. Or, frankly, I use them in the chocolate tiffin every time (page 178)!

Faux chips

There are some lies we tell as parents that are acceptable. The one about the tooth fairy for example. There are some that are not, like insinuating there's pudding and then only producing a mealy apple. That's not pudding in my book. These chips are part of my acceptable lies arsenal. They're frankly delicious and less bad for the heart than the deep-fried variety. They are also what I produce to accompany a lunch with friends.

Serves 1 child as an accompaniment

1 tsp groundnut or sunflower oil
1 medium potato – I like Desiree but use whatever you have to hand

Preheat the oven to 220°C/gas mark 7 and place a pan of water on to boil. Coat a baking tray with the oil and place at the top of the oven to heat.

Now, you can either peel the potato or not. The chips look more aesthetically pleasing when peeled but obviously the fibre and vitamin content is higher if the jackets are left on. Up to you. Once peeled (or not), cut the potato lengthways into slices about 1.5cm thick, then turn these slices on their side and cut into chip shapes, so that they are about 1.5cm thick. Add the potato slices to the pan of boiling water and cook for 5 minutes until the edges are just starting to fluff up and the centres offer only a little resistance when stabbed with a sharp knife. Drain and rest the slices in a sieve over the now empty pan for 2 minutes to help steam off any excess water.

Carefully tip the potato slices onto the baking tray of hot fat, making sure to stand back as they may spit a little. Shake the tray to coat the slices with oil and roast for 10 minutes until golden. Check the centres are completely cooked through and soft by piercing with a knife. Do beware – these retain their heat so cut up and cool a little before serving to small mouths.

These can be spiced up with the addition of a shake of paprika, cumin, pepper or dried rosemary. I consult the kids beforehand if it's solely for their tea.

Rice with peas, broad beans & bacon

This is another one from my husband who is always so much more optimistic about younger palates than I tend to be. Often I come home from work to find the kids tucking into all sorts of concoctions made by Daddy with the help of his mini sous chefs. He's no fish finger serving Daddy, unless they're for him, that is, with lashings of tartare sauce, in a sandwich and post pub.

Serves 2 children

60g white basmati rice
20g frozen broad beans
1 tsp groundnut oil
1 rasher of bacon, chopped into 1cm pieces with scissors
1 tbsp butter
20g frozen peas
Ground black pepper (optional)

In a sieve, rinse the rice in cold water until the water runs clear. Add the rice to a pan filled with plenty of water and bring to a boil. Simmer for 10–12 minutes until cooked through. Drain in a sieve, saving some of the cooking water to boil the broad beans in. Simmer for 5 minutes until cooked through. Drain the beans and remove the tough outer shells if you have the time.

Heat the oil in a frying pan and fry the bacon pieces over a medium heat until crispy. Add the butter, frozen peas and the cooked rice and beans. Gently stir the mixture to coat everything in the oil and allow to heat gently for 5 minutes until the frozen peas are cooked through. Season with black pepper and serve.

Snakes & ladders toast

I have inherited my love of novelty food from my mother. She used to make multi-coloured layered jellies studded with fresh fruit, and buy miniature loaves to conjure into miniature sandwiches for my lunchbox. This is a great way to introduce kids to the wonder that is the world of cheese. You need two different colours, so I'd suggest red Leicester as the orange colour and another paler, yellow cheese that you have to hand.

Toast one side of the bread under the grill. Cut 2 slices off each block of cheese and cut each slice into 3 squares. With the bread toasted side down, arrange the squares of cheese in alternate colours over the slice, to create a pleasing chequerboard effect. Grill until melting and golden. Top with your green pepper snake and use the carrot sticks to fashion a ladder shape.

Ideas for green pepper

Slice finely, roast with sliced onions and sausages and serve with mashed potatoes and gravy. Or use in the enchiladas (page 86) for a tasty way to hoover up any leftover veg. Or slice finely, bag up and freeze, and add frozen strips to curries, soups and stews. Or grill strips on a griddle, and use in a toasted sandwich with goat's cheese and fried tomatoes.

Serves 1

1 slice of bread
Red Leicester cheese
A lighter coloured cheese that
   melts well, like cheddar
A thin slice of green pepper
1 carrot, peeled and sliced
   into thin matchsticks

Mini sticky sausage kebabs

Everything tastes better on a stick. Perhaps it's the association with summertime and parties – beach lollies, smoky barbequed kebabs and, of course, cheese and pineapple hedgehogs. This is a quick dinner I make for the kids that rarely produces any leftovers. They're sticky, they're sweet, they're baked in the oven for minimum effort and they're on cocktail sticks for goodness' sake – what's not to like?!

*Serves 1 child,
scale up as required*

- 1 chipolata sausage, cut into 2cm pieces
- ¼ red pepper, deseeded and chopped into 2cm squares
- 1 tsp honey
- 1 tsp soy sauce
- 1 tsp tomato purée
- Ground black pepper (optional)

About 15 minutes before you plan to make the kebabs pop 2 cocktail sticks into a bowl of cold water and weigh them down with a mug (soaking them will stop them from burning in the oven). Preheat the oven to 220°C/gas mark 7. Line a baking tray with some kitchen foil.

Thread the sausage and pepper pieces onto the soaked sticks and place on the foil-lined baking tray. In a small bowl, mix together the honey, soy sauce, tomato purée and a little pepper and brush it over the kebabs, turning to fully coat. Pour the remaining marinade over the kebabs and bake for 20 minutes until the sausages are browned and cooked through. Serve with rice or strips of tortilla wrap for mopping up the marinade.

Nanny's Yorkshire all-sorts

My mum was the one who introduced my now-addicted youngest son to Yorkshire puddings. It's been a bit of a nightmare getting this recipe out of her as she does everything by eye. Well, no longer! I determinedly watched her with a pen, paper and a set of digital scales. I make mine in silicone cupcake cases as they never stick and need very little lubrication in the form of lard, dripping or oil. They are easy to freeze and are received especially well by children who are addicted to the crunch of rice cakes and breadsticks. Let them choose their own nutritious filling to add to the crunchy receptacle, and everyone's happy.

Makes 12 cupcake-sized Yorkshires

A little lard, groundnut oil
   or beef dripping
100g plain flour
Black pepper (optional)
2 large eggs
175ml whole milk

Preheat the oven to 220°C/gas mark 7 and put a teaspoon of lard, oil or dripping into each of the 12 silicone cupcake cases or metal cupcake tray holes. Place the cases on a baking tray for ease. Transfer the tray to the top shelf of the oven.

Meanwhile, make the batter. Sift the flour into a large bowl, add a pinch of black pepper and make a well in the middle. Crack the eggs into the well and use a whisk (my mum uses a fork, but I just can't get the hang of it) to gradually whisk the flour into the egg until it's very smooth and thick. Gradually add the milk a little at a time, whisking after each addition. Pour the smooth batter into a jug and refrigerate for a minimum of 10 minutes.

When the fat is spitting away and extremely hot – and I mean really hot, for these will not rise if the fat isn't angrily spitting and threatening to scald you – carefully pour the cold batter into each case until half to three-quarters full. Immediately put the tray of cases straight back into the oven, on the top shelf. Leave to rise, with no peeking, for 20–25 minutes or until well risen and golden brown. Take out of the oven and remove from the cases straight away to stop them from soaking up any more of the fat. Serve filled with meat, vegetables, gravy or whatever your son or daughter fancies. Just save one to have with banana and golden syrup for pudding.

Mini mash ups

I once said something utterly ridiculous to my eldest son. He was three at the time and dipping his potato wedges into a glass of milk, sucking the milk off and watching in amazement as potato debris sank to the bottom. An experiment in flavour and physics. All I saw was mess and silliness. I was having a bad day. I confess I said, "You need to grow up Charlie." And I was wrong. He didn't need to, for that comes all too soon. He was only doing what he'd seen Mummy do with a biscuit and a cup of tea. I made a pact with myself not to say anything quite so idiotic again and to make meal times experimental. Here's a suggestion for introducing new foods to children where they control the exploration – there will be wastage but try and see it as an exercise in increasing repertoire. If they don't like mashed potato use rice or cous cous instead.

Serves 1

1 portion of mashed potato
Various foods to mash and
  gobble up, such as: grilled
  bacon, olives, green beans,
  broccoli, baked beans,
  grated cheese, cherry
  tomatoes, ham, roasted
  butternut squash, sliced
  pepper, raw carrots,
  chickpeas, pesto, cooked
  mini sausages...

Have a look in your fridge and pull out anything that could be mashed into the potato. Try not to enforce your own tastes. You may not like broccoli but your offspring might, especially given that they make excellent trees for a mashed potato woodland scene complete with olive bugs. I always explain beforehand that this is still dinnertime, so they need to eat as well as have fun. Put everything you can find into separate little dishes (old yogurt pots are perfect) and let your children pick what they want to mash into the potato at the table.

Baked treasure parcels

There's a sound we hear every day in our house, usually about half an hour before dinnertime. It's a dreadful scraping that, according to every horror film, should signify something bad. But this sound makes my heart sing as it's my youngest pulling a chair across the floor, accompanied by 'Maxi help Mummy?' One day, little Max will grow up and I will be without my very messy, slightly unpredictable and shouty sous chef.

This is one of his favourites and is a great way to get any child excited about eating fish and vegetables. The bonus is that it's not expensive to make. To make things even cheaper, I buy fish fillets on offer, cut them into child-size portions and bag them up individually for the freezer. Just defrost before you use them.

Serves 1 toddler, scale up accordingly

1 tsp olive oil
50g piece of fresh fish like
    salmon or coley
A wedge of lemon
Vegetables of your toddler's
    choice, thinly sliced
Ground black pepper (optional)

Preheat the oven to 190°C/gas mark 5. Take an A4-sized piece of foil. Ask your little one to measure out the oil onto the foil or help them if they find this difficult. Place the fish in the middle of the foil and squeeze over the lemon. Choose vegetables together from the fridge or larder – we tend to discuss each one's colour, texture and flavour – and wash and trim them.

Place the prepared vegetables on top of the fish and sprinkle over a little pepper. Pull the foil together to create a parcel, trying not to squash the package too much as it needs a bit of air to circulate. Place on a baking tray and bake for 15 minutes until the fish is firm and cooked through. Serve the contents of the parcel with bread to dip in the juices or some cous cous.

One of Max's and Charlie's favourite combinations is coley, thinly sliced carrots, frozen peas and a few heads of broccoli.

Ideas for lemon

Place wedges on a greaseproof paper-lined tray, freeze and bag up individually for use in a lemonade or G&T, to add a refreshing citrus hit. Or squeeze some lemon into a mug, add a slice of fresh ginger and drink first thing. Or if your taps are worse for wear, attach a halved lemon to the end of the tap using an elastic band and leave overnight for a chemical-free limescale remover.

DIY fruit (dip it yourself)

An Indian restaurant chain recently opened a new place in Leicester. The opening caused quite a stir. Nothing to do with the delicious spiced meat and vegetable dishes. It was the chocolate fountain that did it, with platters of fruit and marshmallows to freely dip. There is something very enticing about dipping anything into chocolate. This is how meals often end in our house – a little very dark chocolate stirred up into a sauce, for as much as most children are started off on milkier varieties, I think it's useful to get their tastebuds into the good stuff early. It's also higher in iron.

Serves 1, scale up as required

20g good-quality dark chocolate
10ml whole milk
1 tsp butter
Sugar sprinkles
Mini marshmallows
Fruit of your child's choice

Chop or grate the chocolate until fine and place it in a microwaveable bowl with the milk. Heat on high for 30 seconds then give it a little whisk. If it needs longer to melt, pop it back into the microwave on 10 second bursts, but no longer. When molten hot and completely liquid, whisk in the butter.

Serve the sauce in a little pot (like a clean pudding or yoghurt pot) for dipping, with a bowl of sprinkles, a bowl of mini marshmallows and a platter of your child's favourite fruit. Beware – do check the heat of the chocolate sauce before serving to very small children.

Cowboys' & girls' fastest pudding in the west

Years ago when asked to book a very important client lunch by my very important black-rimmed spectacle wearing ad-man boss, I did what any self-respecting 22-year-old girl with a cheap suit and next to no salary might do. I consulted the tome that was the Square Meal directory and chose J Sheekey. This is what I ordered for pudding. It's delicious, it's sweet, it's fruity, it's a little bit like ice cream, it has a great bite to it and best of all for any parent, it's quick and thrifty. Not sure whether cowboys and girls truly carried a freezer but for poetic purposes, they did.

Serves 1, scale up as required

50g frozen berries straight from the freezer (fresh blueberries, raspberries and grapes are all delicious frozen)
25g double cream
25g white chocolate, broken into small pieces

Pop the berries onto the serving plate. Over a very low heat, gently heat the double cream and chocolate in a small saucepan until the chocolate has melted. Be careful not to overheat as white chocolate has a habit of burning very easily. Use a metal spoon to stir the mixture and, when completely combined, pour over the frozen berries. From no pudding in sight to chocolate covered faces in just a matter of minutes!

Ideas for double cream

Keep the kids busy making butter by simply shaking the double cream in a clean jam jar until it separates into butter and buttermilk – add salt to extend the life of the butter or simply freeze it and use the buttermilk in pizza dough (page 182). Or whisk to soft peaks and freeze in ice cube trays, ready for adding to curries, risottos and pasta sauces. Or whisk to medium peaks then fold in a little orange zest and use to sandwich shortbread biscuits, dusted with caster sugar and served with slices of orange. Or, if you're feeling a little glum, then make an adult's version of this pudding by adding a dash of Baileys or Limoncello.

Spotty dog pancakes

Super thin pancakes, the ones you inhale in France, have never been my thing.
I don't know if it's the dainty thinness but they feel insubstantial to me. I know I'm
in the minority. These American-style relations are much more me. Smaller but fatter
and dotted with sultanas, to me they're deeply satisfying. They're great for breakfast
and taste delicious with a little orange or lemon zest added too if you fancy it.

Makes 8 pancakes

130g plain flour
½ tsp bicarbonate of soda
1 tsp baking powder
1 large egg
240ml whole milk with a dash
   of lemon juice added
10g caster sugar
15g butter, melted
100g sultanas
Groundnut or sunflower oil,
   for frying

Place the flour in a large bowl and mix in the bicarbonate of soda and baking powder. In another bowl and using a whisk, beat the egg until frothy. Add the milk and lemon juice mixture, sugar and melted butter to the egg, whisk again and pour over the dry ingredients. Using a metal spoon, mix well until no lumps remain. Add the sultanas and stir through.

Heat 1 tablespoon of oil in a large frying pan over a medium heat. Once the oil starts to sizzle add a ladle of the pancake mixture so that it spreads to about 10cm wide. Once it starts to look firm, between 40 seconds and 2 minutes later (this is dependent on the ferocity of the heat), use a fish slice to flip the pancake over. It should be lightly browned on the flipped side – if it's very dark turn the heat down. Fry on the other side for 40 seconds to 1½ minutes, again depending on the heat. Remove from the pan and wrap in a clean tea towel to keep them warm whilst you make the others. Repeat with the remaining batter.

If you can't eat them all then just place them between layers of greaseproof paper to stop them from sticking and keep them either in the fridge or freezer. These are a real treat when reheated in the microwave for breakfast. Don't save the batter uncooked, as there are too many raising agents added.

Serve with fresh fruit, ice cream, maple syrup or just as they are, as spotty little dogs.

Whizz bang chocolate banana steamed pudding

This won't win any awards for lightness of sponge or indeed presentation! However, sometimes my children ask for a hot pudding as their dinner is being cleared away and not being a woman who has time to steam spotted dick for hours, this is a great alternative. The bowl/mug mechanism of baking seems to tickle the children too.

Measuring here is key, so do crack out the digital scales and measuring spoons rather than doing things by eye. And be sure to use a ripe banana – if you use an unripe one then the cake will not taste banana-y at all.

Serves 2 children generously

45g butter
½ large egg, beaten with a pinch of salt (find ideas for what to do with the other half of the egg below right)
25g caster sugar
5g cocoa powder
40g self-raising flour
¼ tsp bicarbonate of soda
20ml whole milk
1 tsp lime or lemon juice
½ ripe banana (about 50g), mashed very well

In a microwave on high, melt the butter in a microwaveable cereal size bowl or a microwaveable large mug (it needs to be at least 9cm high and 8cm across) for about 1 minute. Add all of the remaining ingredients to the melted butter. Beat vigorously with a fork for 1 minute until everything is well mixed and looks quite smooth.

Place the bowl or mug on a plate in case any of the mixture escapes during cooking, and microwave for 3½ minutes on high. Leave to cool for 5 minutes in the bowl or mug. Taking care as the bowl or mug will still be very hot, use well-wrapped hands to turn the pudding out onto a plate. Cut the pudding in half and serve with whatever adornment is fancied. Be careful of little mouths, as steamed puddings are obviously very hot.

Ideas for beaten egg

Stir through hot pasta along with chopped ham and cooked peas for a very lazy and not very Italian take on carbonara. Or make chicken dippers: soak some raw chicken strips in milk, coat in flour, dip in beaten egg and cover with crunchy cornflakes before baking at 180°C/gas mark 4 for 20 minutes. Or you could just make another steamed chocolate and banana pudding...

I am no wannabe 1950s housewife.
I rarely wear an apron, I can't sew for toffee
and ironing is reserved for shirts and the odd
pair of trousers. I can always think of other things
I'd rather be doing than keeping a spotless house.
However, when it comes to cooking for the one
I love, I'm happy to. Should it be embarrassing to
admit you love to cook for your partner? I don't
think so. We don't do flowers or expensive gifts;
food is how we show our love.

He cooks for me too, at least three nights
of the week, so this isn't about playing the
surrendered wife role. It's about standing up,
loud and proud, whatever your sex, brandishing
a slotted spoon and saying that cooking is love.

And everything here is quick or prepared
ahead and full of flavour. Weeknights are
rushed enough without lengthy recipes.

Dinner for two in a Flash

Garlic mushroom crackle pie

Pies are usually reserved for special occasions in our house, when there's a crowd to witness the crack of the pie lid and offer up plates for second helpings. This pie is not such a spectacle. It's a soothing mushroom stroganoff-inspired pie with a crunch and crackle filo topping. Perfect for a Tuesday night when Friday feels so very far away.

Serves 2

- 1 tbsp groundnut or sunflower oil
- 1 small onion, peeled and finely chopped
- 500g mini portabella mushrooms or whatever you have, sliced
- 2 garlic cloves, peeled and crushed
- A splash of Worcestershire sauce
- 3 tbsp cream cheese
- Ground black pepper
- 2 filo pastry sheets
- 2 tbsp melted butter

Preheat the oven to 200°C/gas mark 6. Heat the oil in a frying pan over a low heat and gently fry the onion for 5 minutes until softened. Turn the heat up to high, add the mushrooms and, giving the mixture an occasional stir, cook for about 10 minutes until the mushrooms have browned and reduced in size by half.

Turn the heat down to low and add the garlic, the Worcestershire sauce, cream cheese and a little black pepper. Stir well and split the mixture between two individual pie dishes. Slightly scrunch the filo sheets and place on top of the filling to cover completely. Brush the pastry with the butter and bake for 10 minutes until the top is lightly brown and crunchy. Serve with green beans and a restorative early night.

Ideas for Worcestershire sauce

Add a dash to cheese on toast for a homely umami hit. Or a little added to beef mince, breadcrumbs, a glug of milk and chopped onions makes for quick and wholesome meatballs. Or mix with tomato ketchup, brown sugar, garlic and red wine vinegar for a flavoursome barbecue marinade. Or adding a dash to a Bloody Mary lifts the humble cocktail to dizzy new heights.

Ideas for filo pastry

Use cooked salmon and cous cous to make mini samosas: just seal the triangles with melted butter and bake at 180°C/gas mark 4 for 20 minutes until brown. Or bake filo triangles of Camembert and pear. Or make little canapé cups; push squares of filo into oiled cupcake trays, brush with melted butter and bake at 200°C/gas mark 6 for 10–15 minutes until brown, and fill with sweetened cream cheese, strawberries and melted chocolate when cool.

Creamily quick crab linguine

Opening a tin automatically seems less effort than sorting through packets of fish from the fridge. It's possibly more trouble to locate the tin opener but the mind works in funny ways. Knowing that the tinned crab will sit there happily for months, nay years, waiting for a dinner opportunity to present itself is part of the appeal.

This is both sweet from the crab meat and hot from the chilli, though tone down the heat if you prefer by replacing the flaked stuff with ½ teaspoon of mild chilli powder. Whatever you do make sure the crab is very well drained. Mushy crab is not a nice thing.

Serves 2

200g dried linguine
2 tbsp groundnut or
    sunflower oil
3 spring onions, finely sliced
2 garlic cloves, peeled
    and crushed
A punnet of cherry tomatoes
    (about 300g)
1 tbsp crème fraîche
170g tin of crab, drained well
1 tsp dried chilli flakes
A handful of breadcrumbs
    (optional)
A handful of fresh flat-leaf
    parsley, roughly chopped
    (optional)

Cook the linguine according to the packet instructions, drain and set aside. Heat the oil in a large pan over a medium heat and add the spring onions, garlic and cherry tomatoes. Fry until the skin of the tomatoes start to split, around 2 minutes. Reduce the heat to low and add the crème fraîche, crab and chilli flakes and stir until well combined and warmed through. Add the cooked pasta, stir and heat for 1 minute.

If crunch is your thing then top the dish with some breadcrumbs and toast under the grill for 2–3 minutes, but it is equally good crunch-free. Scatter with some cooling flat-leaf parsley if you have any, and serve.

Masala lamb chops with cheesy peas

If there were two words to make me giggle they would have to be 'cheesy peas'. Silly sounding, yes, but such a fine accompaniment to a lamb chop that I'm willing to risk sounding like a children's TV presenter in order to dish them up. The name raises a smile but the taste delivers a satisfied silence.

Serves 2

1 tbsp groundnut or
   sunflower oil
1 small onion, peeled and
   finely chopped
1 tsp garam masala (bought or
   homemade, see page 219)
½ tsp cumin seeds
2 lamb chops
Thumbnail-sized piece of fresh
   ginger (about 2cm), peeled
   and grated
3 garlic cloves, peeled
   and crushed
2 tbsp tomato purée
1 tsp ground cayenne
3 tbsp cream cheese
1 tbsp lemon juice
   (bottled is fine)
200g frozen peas
A few coriander leaves,
   for serving

Heat the oil in a frying pan over a medium heat, add the onions and fry until they are starting to brown at the edges. Add the garam masala and cumin seeds and fry for 1 minute before adding the lamb chops. Leave to brown on one side for 3 minutes before turning and repeating on the other.

Mix together the ginger, garlic, tomato purée, cayenne, cream cheese and lemon juice and pour over the chops and into the pan. Turn the heat down to low and leave to bubble for 15 minutes. Add 2 tablespoons of water and the peas, stir and turn the heat up to high for 3 minutes before serving sprinkled with coriander leaves. Serve with rice, roti, naan or a chopped salad.

Ideas for cream cheese

Stir into mashed potato with a little chopped spring onion to perk up bangers and mash. Or mix with icing sugar and lemon zest and spread over digestive biscuits for cheat's-cake. Or spread on rye bread and top with smoked salmon off-cuts, a little lemon juice and a lot of black pepper.

TV dinner miso chicken ramen

Ramen always feels cleansing to me, akin to steaming my face whilst covered in a towel shroud, and this inauthentic version clears your system and restores well-being simultaneously. Please don't worry about the inevitable slurping when eating ramen, it's all part of the process and in Japan, where bona fide ramen hails from, slurping is positively encouraged. Just eat with bowl to your chin, napkin in your collar and slurp away. And if you don't have any leftover chicken, grill a chicken breast or two for 10–15 minutes each side until the juices run clear, then slice finely.

Serves 2

2 large eggs
125g dried noodles,
    such as udon
1 litre chicken stock (for
    quickness this can be made
    from gel stock pots)
18g sachet of miso soup paste
    (I use Wakame)
300g leftover cooked
    chicken, sliced
80g frozen spinach,
    defrosted for 3 minutes
    in the microwave
198g tin of sweetcorn, drained
6 spring onions, sliced
    into rounds

Put the eggs into a small saucepan without a lid and just cover the eggs with cold water. Place on the hob and bring to a boil. Once boiling, reduce to a simmer and put your timer on for 4 minutes. Once cooked, carefully remove the eggs from the pan using a slotted spoon and leave on the side to cool a little whilst still in their shells. Use the leftover hot water to cook the noodles according to their packet instructions.

Heat the stock until simmering and add the miso paste. Stir well. Divide between two bowls then assemble the ramen like a clock face. Fill one quarter with chicken, another with spinach, the third with sweetcorn and the final with noodles. Peel the eggs, cut in half lengthways and place two halves in each bowl. Top with the spring onions and slurp to your heart's content.

Virtuous soy & ginger salmon

Salmon always feels a little virtuous to me. Perhaps it's the gentle baby pink colour once cooked, or the happy coupling with other clean flavours like steamed rice or green vegetables. So it's a perfect midweek supper I'd say, all lean and clean and putting a little credit in your bank for a more indulgent weekend. That's not to say this isn't a delicious end to a Wednesday, it most certainly is. You're halfway there.

Serves 2

30g brown sugar
10g fresh ginger,
    peeled and grated
40ml cold water
15ml light soy sauce
15ml fish sauce
15ml lime juice (bottled is fine)
1 tbsp groundnut or
    sunflower oil
2 salmon fillets

Place the sugar, ginger and water in a small saucepan and boil for 3 minutes until the sugar has dissolved. Remove the pan from the heat and add the soy sauce, fish sauce and the lime juice. Stir well.

Heat the oil in a frying pan over a medium heat and add the salmon. Fry until you can see the bright pink flesh change to a lighter colour halfway up the fillet, then, using a fish slice, flip each fillet over. Pour the sauce over the fish and when the salmon is light pink throughout and cooked through (the time is dependent on the thickness of the fillets) remove the fillets from the pan. Turn the heat up under the pan and reduce the liquid down for about 1 minute to a sticky sauce. Pour the sauce over the fish and serve immediately with fluffy basmati rice, steamed greens, or if you're feeling a bit naughty, fried noodles.

Blue cheese burgers without the buns

Somehow removing the buns makes these burgers seem less of a junk food treat and more of a midweek supper. I'm not sure why. Perhaps it's the necessity to use a knife and fork with the bun removed? Of course you could serve them in a bun, it matters not. Use any cheese you like for the centres, it's just that for me, blue cheese and beef are a perfect match. Add a glass of red wine and this would be fit for a last supper.

The bread in the burger mixture binds it all together and helps to stop the cheese from seeping out but you can leave it out, just use another half an egg if you do.

Serves 2

250g good-quality steak mince
1 large egg
½ slice of white bread, broken into 1cm pieces
Ground black pepper
40g blue cheese (or other squashable cheese)
1 tsp vegetable oil

You need a very hot pan to fry these burgers. You can also use a grill but I find the heat easier to achieve with a pan, plus there's the added bonus of being able to squash the burgers down with a spatula to achieve that chargrilled appearance.

Preheat the oven to 190°C/gas mark 5. Place the mince in a large bowl and add the egg, bread and season well with pepper. Roll your sleeves up and use clean hands to squish the meat until the pepper, egg and bread are well distributed. Take half the mince mixture and roll into a ball. Split the cheese in half and fashion half the cheese into a square shape about 4 x 4cm. Squash the cheese into the middle of the burger, then shape the meat around the cheese, squashing as you go to ensure there is a good seal. It's not the end of the world if the cheese escapes during frying, but it does somewhat ruin the surprise.

Heat the oil in a frying pan over a high heat and, once the pan is very hot, slip the burgers into it. Use a spatula to push the burgers down gently and when they are looking chargrilled on the bottom, about 3–4 minutes, flip the burgers over and repeat on the other side for the same amount of time. Finish off in the oven until the burgers are cooked through, about 10 minutes for well done, 5 minutes for medium rare, then serve with a watercress salad or, if you're feeling devilish, a side of faux chips (page 44) and a bun. Ketchup, mustard and mayonnaise are all optional.

Hot & smoky tomato prawns with sticky coconut rice

Prawns are forever a decadent supper in my mind due to the much-loved prawn cocktail enjoyed on rare trips out to restaurants as a child. Prawns smothered in Marie Rose sauce and served up on crunchy cold iceberg lettuce still have a place in my heart, but this is what I crave after a long day.

Serves 2

150g white basmati rice
8 tomatoes, cut in half
1 tbsp groundnut oil
1 tsp smoked paprika
1 tsp salt
20g block of creamed coconut, grated
190g raw peeled prawns
1 red chilli, sliced
A handful of fresh coriander (optional)

Soak the rice in a measuring jug of cold water. Meanwhile, preheat the oven to 150°C/gas mark 2 and put the tomatoes in a roasting tin and sprinkle with oil and paprika. Cook on the middle shelf of the oven for 30 minutes until well roasted.

Now it's action stations. Drain the rice in a sieve and rinse it in cold water, to get rid of the excess starch that can make your rice stodgy, until the water runs clear. Return the rice to the measuring jug and make a note of the volume in millilitres. Tip into a saucepan and add double the amount of cold water to rice. Stir in the salt and coconut. Bring to the boil without a lid then reduce the heat to a low simmer, cover with a lid and leave to cook for 10 minutes. Don't peek – the lid needs to stay on throughout. I set a timer for this, as rice is precise stuff.

Meanwhile, add the prawns and chilli to the tomato mixture, shake a little and return to the oven for 10 minutes. Once the rice timer goes, remove the rice pan from the heat and leave with the lid on for 5 minutes. Once cooked, fluff the rice up with a fork and serve it with the hot prawns poured over the top. Snip over some coriander if you have some.

Ideas for creamed coconut

Put half a block of coconut cream, a tin of tomatoes, a tin of cold water, 2 tins of chickpeas and a tablespoon each of turmeric, garam masala, ground cumin and ground coriander into a pan and simmer for 10 minutes, then add a crushed garlic clove for a quick veggie curry. Or add 75g grated creamed coconut to a basic sponge for a tropical change and couple with fresh mango and desiccated coconut spiked cream for a showstopper.

Chuck it in the tin butternut squash, chorizo & butter bean soup

I made this for a foodie trade fair where I was required to cook and bake for 12 hours straight each day. Hugely daunted by the prospect of feeding hordes of buyers looking for the perfect garlic crusher to bestow upon their customers, I did what any sensible girl might have done and introduced chorizo to the equation. This soup was snaffled faster than I could whizz it up with the stick blender. Me, well I love it because it delivers chorizo-flavoured punch without the texture, which I've never been too keen on.

Makes 2 huge servings or 4 normal ones

- ½ butternut squash (about 375g once prepared), peeled, deseeded and cut into 3cm cubes
- 2 medium onions (about 150g in total), peeled and quartered
- 1 tsp groundnut or vegetable oil
- 225g chorizo sausage, cut into slices (skin removed if you have time)
- 1 chicken stock cube, crumbled
- 1 tsp ground black pepper
- 800ml boiling water
- 410g tin of butter beans, drained and rinsed

Preheat the oven to 200°C/gas mark 6. Chuck everything except for the butter beans and the water into a roasting tin and roast in the oven for 30 minutes until the butternut squash is tender.

Tip everything from the roasting tin into a large saucepan, add the water and blend with a stick blender until smooth. If you don't have a stick blender pour the mixture into a food processor, whizz until smooth and pour back into the saucepan. Turn the heat to low, add the butter beans and cook for 5 minutes until heated through. Serve with some bread, which can be spread with a little harissa paste if you're a heat fiend.

Ideas for butternut squash

Roast cubes of squash for 30 minutes at 200°C/gas mark 6 then mash up and add some black pepper, salt and chopped coriander to make a slightly sweet mash. Or try making a speedy cheat's Thai curry using a bought paste – just fry off the paste with some onions, add some cubed squash and a tin of coconut milk, simmer for 20 minutes until the squash is tender and add a handful of frozen peas to cook off right at the end.

The Guerrilla Gardener's Baghdad beef stew

I had the good fortune to work with Richard Reynolds, aka The Guerrilla Gardener, on the *Financial Times* advertising account when he was just starting out, saving the world one dig at a time. One evening he invited myself and some other ad pals for dinner and made this. I think I ate three bowls. This is the recipe as I imagine it, though rather less sweet and nutty than the original. It's a slow cooker stew so pop it in on Sunday, let it sit overnight in the fridge and it'll be even better by Monday evening. It also freezes well.

Serves 6

2 tbsp groundnut oil
500g stewing or braising steak, cut into 3–4cm chunks
2 tsp ground cinnamon
2 large carrots, peeled and sliced
3 medium onions, peeled and finely sliced
1 tsp ground black pepper
60ml white wine vinegar
40g honey
750ml boiling water
1 beef stock cube, crumbled
150g raisins
100g flaked almonds
415g tin of figs, drained, or 150g dried figs, chopped

Heat the oil in a frying pan over a medium heat and brown the beef on all sides. Add the cinnamon, stir to mix and fry for 2 minutes. Spoon it all into your slow cooker or a casserole dish with a lid.

Place the carrots, onions, pepper, vinegar and honey in with the beef. Make the stock by pouring the water over the stock cube and stir until dissolved. Add the stock to the beef and cook in the slow cooker on the low setting or in a 140°C/gas mark 1 oven for 6 hours. It's ready when the beef easily falls apart.

Ladle the stew into a container and add the raisins, flaked almonds and figs, give it a stir and leave overnight. Come the next night you'll find the raisins have absorbed a lot of the liquid – simply reheat on the stove or in the microwave. I serve it with basmati rice or quinoa.

Lemony salmon pasta with courgettes & peas

Before I had children I wasted so much time, I faffed about. Procrastination was my middle name. Once I lived without any bedroom curtains for a summer because I couldn't find the time to choose some. Well, what a fool I was. Now when I see friends pregnant with their first child I plead with them to get all those niggling little jobs done. For once that baby is out time evaporates. It slips away, though happily I might add. Any parent will testify that the days are long but the years are short.

Here's a pasta dish for when 20 minutes is all you can spare at the end of a long day, whether you have children or not.

Serves 2

200g conchiglie pasta
   (or whatever is in your
   cupboard, but these hold
   the salmon very nicely)
75g salted butter
1 courgette, cut in half
   lengthways and then
   into half moons
100g frozen peas
Finely grated zest and
   juice of 1 lemon
120g pack of smoked salmon
   slices or trimmings, torn
   into pieces if large
50g Parmesan, grated
Ground black pepper

Cook the pasta according to the packet instructions. Meanwhile, melt the butter in a frying pan over a low heat and add the courgette, peas and the lemon zest and juice. Fry until the courgettes have sucked up all that buttery, lemony goodness and the peas look soft and cooked through; this should only take about 5 minutes. Stir in the smoked salmon and remove the pan from the heat.

When the pasta is cooked, drain well and add to the frying pan. Stir well to coat all the pasta with the sauce and let the residual heat warm through the smoked salmon. Split between serving dishes, top with the Parmesan and black pepper and enjoy.

Supper served in 20 minutes flat.

'Bring out your leftovers' baked chicken enchiladas

Here's a very quick Monday night dinner that's perfect for the day after the hearty family Sunday roast. The amount of chicken is irrelevant — in fact these enchiladas are still lovely and filling when served vegetarian style. We use these to hoover up any veggies in need of sacrifice, so the ones below are just a suggestion. This will make dinner for tonight and another portion for tomorrow.

Serves 2, twice

2 tbsp vegetable, hemp
   or groundnut oil
1 red onion, peeled
   and sliced
1 pepper, deseeded and sliced
2 garlic cloves, peeled
   and crushed
400g tin of chopped tomatoes
1 tsp chilli powder
1 tsp ground cumin
Leftover cooked chicken
   (at least 1 breast or leg),
   shredded
400g tin of black eyed beans,
   drained
325g tin of sweetcorn, drained
6 tortilla wraps
150g half-fat crème fraîche
75g strong cheese such as
   cheddar, grated
Ground black pepper
A handful of fresh coriander,
   chopped (optional)

Preheat the oven to 180°C/gas mark 4. Grease 2 ovenproof dishes that are as wide as the tortillas with 1 tablespoon of the oil. Heat the remaining oil in a large frying pan over a moderate heat. Fry the onion for 5 minutes until it starts to brown slightly, then add the pepper slices and garlic and fry for 2 more minutes. Add the tomatoes, chilli and cumin and reduce to a low heat. Gently cook for 5 minutes.

Stir through the cooked chicken, black eyed beans and sweetcorn. Leave to heat through for 15 minutes, allowing the sauce to reduce a little. Remove the pan from the heat and spoon a sixth of the mixture into the centre of each tortilla. Wrap each tortilla up like a cigar, leaving both ends open, and place 3 in each dish, with the 'join' facing downwards. Mix the crème fraîche with the cheese and some black pepper and spread over the top of the enchiladas. Bake for 30 minutes. Serve scattered with coriander and a crunchy side salad if you like.

When I worked in advertising, I once had a client who had a barbecue every Christmas Eve come rain, shine or snow. He explained in clipped dulcet tones that one shouldn't let the weather get in the way of eating. Which is a fine mantra for life. Though he had served in the Gulf so he could be described as more fearless than your average barbecuing Joe.

Eating outside is a pleasure in my eyes. Whether standing, teeth chattering and zipped up in a ski jacket at the park armed with a flask of tea and a slice of cake or in a strappy vest, sunglasses and with the billowing smoke of a just lit barbecue in the back garden, I just love eating outside. Everything tastes better with a little vitamin D soaking through the clouds and into your skin.

Of course anything can be eaten outside, but these are things I like to take on picnics, to barbecues or simply eat in the garden when the sun is shining. Most of them are deliberately summery in theme; I like to think they might entice the sun out, but that may well be wishful thinking.

Food for the Great Outdoors

Picnic loaf

This is bread designed especially with a picnic in mind. The inspiration behind it was the original Cornish pasty, a savoury filling at one end and sweet at the other. Add a massive hunk of cheese and some red fruits for a two-course meal to be washed down with your Enid Blyton picnic beverage of choice. Lashings of fiery ginger beer in my case, and very cold non-ginger beer in my husband's.

Serves 3 for lunch

For the dough:

250g strong white flour, plus a little extra for dusting

30g butter

125ml whole or semi-skimmed milk

5g fast action dried yeast

6g salt, plus a little extra for the egg wash

20g caster sugar

2 large eggs

1 tbsp olive oil

For the savoury filling:

1 small onion, peeled and finely chopped

1 tbsp butter

1 tbsp groundnut or sunflower oil

A pinch of salt

1 slice of Parma ham, chopped into 2cm pieces

For the sweet filling:

1 tbsp chocolate hazelnut spread

Preheat the oven to 180°C/gas mark 4 and place a rack in the middle of the oven. Tip the flour into an ovenproof bowl and place in the oven for 2 minutes – the warmth will help an enriched dough like this to rise.

Melt the butter in a saucepan. Add the milk and heat on the hob until warm but still cool enough to pop your finger in. Remove from the heat. Add the yeast, salt and sugar to the warm flour, stir and then tip in the milk and butter and stir again. Add one egg and stir well. Cover a work surface with the oil and knead (see page 133) for 5–10 minutes until smooth and elastic. Pop the dough into the warmed bowl and cover with cling film.

Meanwhile, prepare the savoury filling by frying the onions over a low heat in the butter, oil and salt until soft and caramelised. Remove from the heat and tip onto some kitchen roll or a clean tea towel to remove any excess fat. Add the ham to the onion.

When the dough has doubled, lightly flour the work surface and knead very lightly for 1–2 minutes. Shape into a rectangle about 24cm in length. Roll to about a 1cm thickness. Keep pulling the dough up from the work surface, allowing it to shrink back a little after each couple of rolls.

Lightly spread half the dough with chocolate spread, and sprinkle the other half with the fried onion and ham, leaving a small gap around the edges and between the sweet and savoury fillings. Fold over the two edges of dough that have both types of filling running along them, so that they meet in the middle and none of the filling can be seen. Pinch the middle edges and the ends together well so that it is completely sealed.

You will now need to repeat the process by folding the long edges into the middle again; this is important as it will stop the

Stuff a little blue cheese into dried dates and wrap in thin strips of Parma ham for a sweet and salty canapé. Or make a mammoth French bread toastie for all the family (see page 18). Or lay on a plate, add torn mozzarella and some fresh basil and drizzle with balsamic reduction and olive oil for an easy at home lunch or a decadent desk lunchbox. Or wrap around chicken breasts stuffed with herby cream cheese and bake for 25–30 minutes at 200°C/gas mark 6, for a low maintenance, high flavour, weeknight supper.

filling from escaping when it is baking. Pinch the long edges together again, really squashing the dough as you pinch to produce a seal.

Turn the baton so it is seal side down and use your hands to push under the dough and create a taut, smooth top. Ensure the ends are sealed by pinching the dough, and transfer to a floured baking tray. Sprinkle with flour and loosely cover with cling film.

Once the dough has doubled in size (this takes about 45 minutes in a warm kitchen but will take longer if it's really cold) preheat the oven to 220°C/gas mark 7. Make the egg wash by beating the second egg with a pinch of salt. Paint the wash over the loaf, being careful that it doesn't run down and stick the loaf to the baking tray. Slash the loaf lengthways in 3 long lines using a very sharp knife. Be careful not to slash too deeply to expose the filling. Place in the oven then after 2 minutes turn the oven down to 200°C/gas mark 6. After 20 minutes remove the loaf from the tray and bake directly on the oven shelf rack. The bread is ready after another 5–10 minutes, when it is a dark golden brown and hollow sounding. (This bread will colour quickly and darkly due to the high sugar content – don't be alarmed!) Remove from the oven and leave to cool on a wire rack.

Spritely pepper prawn skewers

The sweetness of the fizz combined with the sweet prawn meat and zingy citrus makes these a very moreish skewer. My hatred for waste extends even to the defunct lemon and lime here, but only use lemon zest — the lime zest will push the marinade over to the wrong side of zesty.

Makes 4 skewers

For the skewers:

Finely grated zest and
   juice of 1 lemon
Juice of 1 lime
2cm piece of fresh ginger,
   peeled and grated
500ml lemonade
300g raw and peeled
   large prawns
1 red pepper, deseeded
   and cut into 2cm squares

For the melon salsa:

½ small cantaloupe melon,
   peeled
10 cherry tomatoes, halved
½ red onion, peeled and cut
   into 1cm cubes
A little finely grated
   orange zest

Soak 4 wooden skewers in water for 15 minutes, weighing them down with a mug or bowl. This will stop them from burning during cooking.

Mix together the lemon zest, lemon and lime juices, ginger and lemonade in a flat dish that will fit the skewers. Cut the deflated lemon and lime halves into four pieces and thread these, the prawns and pepper alternately onto the skewers. Place in the marinade and leave for 2 hours, overnight if possible.

Remove from the marinade and grill on the barbecue or under a hot grill for 5 minutes until cooked through. I serve these with a melon salsa; dice the melon into 1cm cubes and mix with the tomatoes, red onion and orange zest.

Backyard chargrilled carrot salad

Our first married abode was a tall terrace at the top of the hill, overlooking the city. I remember obsessing over a garden the whole time we lived there. If only I had a garden rather than a slab of concrete then life would be complete. Well now I have a little garden and find myself thinking about other things I might want. There's a lesson for me in this; to count blessings and appreciate the present. Trite and a little smug sounding but important stuff. This is a salad we used to eat in our perfectly serviceable yard when friends came over for lunch.

Serves 4
as a side salad

365g carrots (about 5 medium ones), trimmed and peeled
15ml groundnut oil
100g sultanas
45ml fresh orange juice
30g fresh coriander
20g flaked almonds

I cut my carrots lengthways using a mandolin. I love the rhythmic action and pleasing skinniness of the slices. But a knife will do the job with a steady hand. You want your long slices to be as thin as possible. Coat the carrots in the groundnut oil and chargrill on a very hot griddle pan, a few at a time. A frying pan also works fine but there'll be no griddle marks. You're aiming to just mark the carrots before placing them into a waiting serving dish, so only griddle for a scant minute on each side.

Meanwhile, heat the sultanas in a small saucepan with the orange juice until almost all the liquid is absorbed. Add this to the serving dish. Sprinkle the fresh coriander into the serving dish and toss it all together using clean hands. Top with the flaked almonds and serve whilst still slightly warm and before the coriander wilts.

Soothing rosemary & walnut pockets filled with cheese

These are fast food bread pockets, at least fast for the bread world. Homemade bread is more the tortoise in the great feeding race but this variety is so much faster than others due to the fast rising spelt flour and short second prove. Spelt often loses its shape when baked in traditional loaf form so flat pockets are the perfect vehicle for it. Thoughtfully pre-flattened into a scooping device, these are perfect for mopping up marinades and salad remnants, as well as being welcome receptacles for chargrilled meats. They are also perfectly satisfying alone; the melted cheese sees to that.

Makes 8

500g strong brown spelt flour, plus extra for dusting
10g salt
7g fast action dried yeast
40ml olive oil
280ml warm water
100g walnuts, finely chopped
3 tbsp chopped fresh rosemary
150g taleggio cheese, grated

Ideas for taleggio

Cut into cubes and toss in just-drained pasta topped with fried portabella mushrooms and a good bit of black pepper. Or take advantage of taleggio's melting properties and make quesadillas: thinly slice the cheese and place between tortilla wraps along with fresh spinach leaves, then fold and fry in a teaspoon of olive oil.

Mix together the flour, salt, yeast, oil and water in a large bowl then knead (see page 133 for instructions on how to knead) until smooth and elastic. Put back in the bowl, cover with cling film and leave to prove until doubled in size.

Preheat the oven to 220°C/gas mark 7 and line 2 baking trays with non-stick greaseproof paper. Knock the dough back, using your hands to deflate, then add the walnuts and rosemary and knead until evenly distributed. Form the dough into a sausage shape on a lightly floured surface and cut into 8 pieces. Roll each out into a long oval shape about 5mm thick, sprinkle half the oval with cheese then fold in half and use a little water to seal the edges. Squash the edges together tightly with your fingers – this is a really important step as otherwise the cheese will escape whilst baking. Place on the prepared baking trays and leave to prove for 5 minutes.

Bake for 10 minutes until puffed up and browned.

Tortilla traybake

If a picnic food is to stink out the whole car it must be a delicious, welcome aroma. For as much as I adore an egg mayonnaise and cress sandwich I don't want to share air with it on a long journey, such is its infectious nature. This tortilla traybake, however, is the perfect road trip companion. Yes it contains egg but there's no unpleasant odour. Just piggy chorizo and fried onions; it's almost the fug of the fairground. And the best bit – if you line the tray with foil there's no washing up to ferry home.

Serves 6–8

4 tbsp olive oil
200g chorizo sausage, thinly sliced
2 large onions (about 280g in total), peeled and thinly sliced
4 garlic cloves, peeled and crushed
½ tsp salt
1 red pepper, deseeded and thinly sliced
3 medium potatoes (about 300g in total), peeled and very thinly sliced
5 large eggs
Ground black pepper

Preheat the oven to 190°C/gas mark 5 and line a 25 x 18cm ovenproof dish or tray with foil or parchment lined foil. Heat 3 tablespoons of the oil in a non-stick pan and fry the chorizo, onions, garlic, salt and red pepper for about 5 minutes until starting to brown. Use a slotted spoon to remove the onions and peppers from the pan and place in the foil-lined dish. Add the remaining tablespoon of oil to the pan and fry the potatoes for 5 minutes, coating the slices in the oil well. Pour all of the mixture into the foil-lined dish. Use a spoon to mix the ingredients so that they're evenly distributed, but be careful not to stab a hole in the foil.

Beat the eggs in a bowl with the black pepper and pour over the chorizo and vegetable mix. Use your spoon to encourage the egg to distribute evenly, then bake for 20–25 minutes or until the egg is firm and the top of the tortilla is brown. If there are any leftovers, this is an excellent lunchbox surprise.

Mark's moreish roasted vegetable, lentil & halloumi salad with bacon rashers

I've been best mates with my pal Georgie for many years. I first spied her at sixth form college, all pale and interesting with curly wurly hair like Andie MacDowell, the heroine of my favourite film of the 90s, *Four Weddings and a Funeral*. Georgie didn't marry a Hugh lookalike, more a Mr. Darcy. His name is even Mark and he's a mean cook. This is his much-asked-for recipe.

Serves 4

2 red onions, peeled
1 red pepper, deseeded
2 courgettes
½ butternut squash, peeled and deseeded
2 sweet potatoes, peeled
8 tomatoes
300g mushrooms
1 tsp ground black pepper
1 tsp smoked paprika
1 sprig of rosemary, needles only
2 tbsp olive oil
4 bacon rashers
410g tin of green lentils, drained
250g halloumi, cut into 2cm cubes

For the dressing:

1 tbsp white wine vinegar
1 tsp Dijon mustard
3 tbsp olive oil
1 garlic clove, peeled and crushed
½ tsp salt
½ tsp ground black pepper

Preheat the oven to 180°C/gas mark 4. Cut all the vegetables into about 2cm cubes and add to a large roasting tin. Season with the pepper, paprika, rosemary and oil. Roast for 20–25 minutes until soft and golden looking.

Meanwhile, grill the bacon until crispy, about 6–8 minutes, then chop into 2cm pieces. Once cooked, remove the vegetables from the oven and stir through the chopped bacon and lentils. Place the cubes of halloumi on top and return the tin to the oven for about 10 minutes until the cheese has started to brown.

Meanwhile, make the dressing by shaking all the ingredients in a jam jar until blended – this will take about a minute.

Remove the roasting tin from the oven, tip into a serving dish and either eat hot drizzled with dressing or allow to cool, drizzle with the dressing and serve with salads and grilled meats.

Suffolk smoke house tart with mustard seed pastry

Every year we travel down to the Suffolk coast for our summer holiday. The main focus of the trip is to eat as much pork, cider, apples, smoked fish and cheeses, oysters and asparagus (if we hit the right time of year) as possible. This is a tart I make using all the smoky goodies I can get my hands on from Richardson's Smoke House in Orford.

Serves 8

For the pastry:
280g plain flour, plus extra
   for dusting
140g cold salted butter,
   cut into 1cm cubes
2 tbsp mustard seeds
55ml icy cold water
Or
500g shortcrust pastry

For the filling:
200g new potatoes
½ tsp dried dill
140g smoked cheese such
   as Applewood, grated
2 large eggs, lightly beaten
200ml half-fat crème fraîche
Ground black pepper
300g smoked fish like
   mackerel, kipper or haddock,
   skin removed and broken
   into 3cm chunks

Make the pastry. Place the flour in a bowl and stir in the butter using a blunt knife, until all the pieces are well coated. Wash your hands in cold water and rub the butter into the flour until you have a very fine breadcrumb-like consistency. Stir in the mustard seeds, then use the blunt knife to mix, adding enough icy water to just pull the pastry together (you may not need all of it, just use enough to pull it together but not so much that it's sticky). Wrap in cling film and chill for 20 minutes.

Boil the potatoes for 10–15 minutes until tender, then plunge into cold water. When they're cool enough to handle, drain and slice into 5mm-thick rounds. Beat together the dill, cheese, eggs, crème fraîche and pepper in a jug and gently mix in the fish.

On a lightly floured work surface, roll the chilled pastry into a circle shape, about 30cm wide and as thick as a pound coin. Place your flat hands, palm face up and fingers spread wide, under the circle and transfer it to a 22cm loose-bottomed tart tin. Push the pastry into the edges of the tin and run the rolling pin over the top to trim any excess pastry. Chill for 15 minutes. Re-roll the pastry trimmings and bake them to eat with cheese.

Preheat the oven to 190°C/gas mark 5. Line the pastry with greaseproof paper and fill with baking beans, uncooked rice or dried beans. Blind bake for 15 minutes, then remove the beans and paper and return to the oven for 10 minutes or until it looks entirely cooked through. Give the fish mixture another stir and pour into the case. Top with the potato slices and bake for 20–25 minutes, until browned and a knife inserted shows no wet filling.

Salty & fragrant lamb steaks

Some things sound so wrong they're right. Telling my friends and family I'd decided to marry a man I'd only known for nine days and that we were planning on trying for a baby immediately sounded wrong, some may say a bit foolish, but it felt so right. Fish and lamb don't sound like natural bedfellows, but they are! You won't notice the fish, I promise, other than to add a rich depth of saltiness that regular salt doesn't achieve.

Serves 4

2 anchovies in oil
1 tsp chopped fresh
    rosemary or ½ tsp dried
10 garlic cloves,
    peeled and crushed
2 tbsp olive oil
4 lamb steaks

Blend the anchovies, the rosemary, garlic and oil in a food processor or with a stick blender until smooth. Tenderise the meat by bashing the steaks with a meat cleaver or rolling pin. Place the steaks in a freezer bag with the marinade, squeeze the air out of it and seal closed. Refrigerate until ready to grill or barbecue, ideally overnight.

For a medium rare steak you will need to grill the lamb for 2 minutes on each side on a very hot grill or barbecue; for well done you will need 4 minutes on each side. I serve this with lots of broccoli and thick, crunchy-skinned jacket potatoes.

Ideas for anchovies

Anchovies keep in olive oil for a long time; just pop them in the fridge and don't worry if the oil solidifies – this is only due to the low temperature of the fridge, the anchovies remain fine. Or mash up a few anchovies with leftover fresh herbs like parsley or basil, add crushed garlic, some sliced olives and a little lemon juice and spread over bread before toasting under the grill. Or add a few finely chopped anchovies to a pan with a 400g tin of tomatoes, a slug of olive oil, a little garlic and a tablespoon of sugar and simmer very gently for an hour; serve stirred into pasta with a little grated Parmesan on top.

Goat's cheese, mint & broad bean pâté on chilli toasts

I am a huge fan of the canapé, but only when other people are making them.
When faced with the task myself I come over all grumpy teenager, feeling my
limbs grow heavy and my arms stretch to the ground in expected repetitive boredom.
But these are easy to assemble, requiring little finesse. In fact, if you're feeling extra
lazy simply leave a bowl of the pâté out with some mini toasts and finely chopped
chilli. Voilà – canapés for guests to assemble themselves!

Makes 23-30 toasts

For the chilli toasts:
1 red chilli
3 tbsp olive oil
1 French stick

For the pâté:
300g tin of broad beans,
  drained (165g when
  drained)
3 mint leaves, roughly chopped
100g goat's cheese, broken
  into small pieces
1 garlic clove, peeled
  and crushed
3 tbsp olive oil
3 tbsp lemon juice
Ground black pepper

Make the chilli toasts by whizzing the chilli and olive oil in
a small food processor or with a stick blender until finely
chopped and well mixed. Pop into a bowl. Slice the French
stick thinly and toast on both sides.

Roughly mash all the pâté ingredients together so that a little
texture remains, spread it over the toasts and top with a drizzle
of the chilli oil. Or leave everything in individual bowls for people
to help themselves.

Burger relish style coleslaw

It always amazes me the number of people who profess not to like cabbage and yet inhale coleslaw come the summer. Here's my family recipe for coleslaw. It's a little carroty and appley sweet, a little peppery from the radish, has the all-important onion sting and the zest cuts through the mayonnaise. It is the perfect accompaniment to any type of burger through inclusion of the sesame seeds. It's almost a burger bun, but not quite.

Serves 8

¼ red cabbage (about 400g)
1 red onion, peeled
10 radishes, trimmed
3 large carrots, trimmed
  and peeled
1 tsp salt
3 apples (I use Granny Smith
  for their crunch), cored
Finely grated zest and
  juice of 1 lemon
5 tbsp mayonnaise
2 tbsp sesame seeds

Finely shred the cabbage, red onion and radishes into strips. I use my food processor but a sharp knife and a little time spent concentrating on even cutting and you'll have the same result. Grate the carrots and place these, the cabbage, red onion and radishes in a colander over the sink and sprinkle with salt. Leave for 40 minutes to drain away any excess liquid.

Just before serving, finely shred the apples and tip into a serving bowl. Add the lemon zest and juice and toss well. Stir in the vegetables and the mayonnaise until evenly distributed. Sprinkle with the sesame seeds and serve.

Ideas for sesame seeds

If you've never tried dukkah (page 216) then please do as it is delicious and so moreish it should have a health warning for addiction. Or try steaming some broccoli and sprinkling with fresh lemon juice and sesame seeds for a healthy dressing with added calcium. Or make a Japanese-style dressing by mixing sesame seeds with crushed garlic, rice vinegar and soy sauce, to drizzle over crunchy salads and fish.

Orzo & minted pea pasta salad

Normally, if a recipe for a pasta salad mandates the type of pasta, I automatically disregard it in a red mist. Who are they to tell me what pasta to use? Unless they're Italian of course and then I just shut up and do what I'm told. Anyway, I'm about to do the same thing and say it's really worth hunting for orzo. Little grains of pasta that work really well with the frozen petit pois simply because they're the same size. If you can't find them just choose small pasta shapes of your choice.

This is a little taste of summer whatever the weather and perfect with barbequed lamb or indeed on a picnic with some falafel. It's easy, to boot.

Serves 4–6
as a side dish

160g orzo pasta
70g frozen petit pois
1 tbsp olive oil
1 tsp ground black pepper
2 tbsp lemon juice
1 tbsp white wine vinegar
15 mint leaves, very finely
    chopped

Boil the pasta according to the packet instructions then, just before you are about to drain it, add the frozen peas. Give them a stir and leave, in the boiling water, but not on the hob, for 1 minute. Drain the pasta and peas in a sieve and run under the cold tap for 2 minutes to stop the peas from overcooking. Transfer to a serving dish and stir in the remaining ingredients. Serve immediately or refrigerate and serve chilled.

Ideas for mint

Chop up some mint along with parsley and add to boiled, cooled bulgar wheat along with lemon juice, olive oil and chopped tomatoes for a quick tabbouleh. Or finely chop and stir through vanilla ice cream along with chocolate chips for a retro classic. Or pop in a mug, pour boiling water over and add sugar to taste for a caffeine-free, digestion-aiding end to a gluttonous evening.

Holiday hammock pecan & date loaf

I am slightly addicted to women's magazines. I love the recipes, but most of all I love the travel and lifestyle section where there's an interview and nose around some wonderful woman's holiday home in a hot climate. Now that's the life I aspire to. This cake is what I would bring if ever invited to stay. It is also a mighty fine way to finish off a picnic.

Please note that this is a treacley cake. I know this sounds obvious, but don't make it unless you love that slightly bitter taste. That doesn't mean it's an 'adult cake' — far from it. Though maybe replace the Malibu with lemon if it's for a mixed age crowd.

110g salted butter, plus
    extra for greasing
80g treacle
150g golden syrup
250ml whole milk
110g dark muscovado sugar
230g self-raising flour
1 tsp bicarbonate of soda
1 tsp ground ginger
1 tsp ground cinnamon
100g dates (about 15), each
    chopped into about 6 pieces
80g pecans, each chopped into
    about 4 pieces
1 large egg
150g icing sugar
60g desiccated coconut
40ml Malibu rum, or lemon
    juice if you're going
    booze free

Ideas for dates

Add chopped dates to spinach leaves with toasted almonds and fried onions for a side salad. Or stuff with a little blue cheese, wrap in some bacon, bake for 25 minutes at 180°C/gas mark 4 and serve with Prosecco.

Preheat the oven to 180°C/gas mark 4 and grease and line a 2lb loaf tin, about 22 x 12cm, 6cm deep. In a large saucepan (and it must be large as you will be adding lots of ingredients to this pan), heat the butter, treacle, golden syrup, milk and dark muscovado sugar over a low heat until everything has melted and dissolved. You can give it a few stirs with a wooden spoon to help it along.

Meanwhile, in a bowl, stir together the flour, bicarbonate of soda, ginger and cinnamon until well distributed. Add the chopped dates and pecans and stir again until everything is thoroughly coated in the spiced flour mixture.

When the treacle mixture has dissolved, remove the pan from the heat and tip the flour mixture into it. Beat well with a wooden spoon until any lumps have disappeared. Add the egg and beat again. The batter will be glossy and very dark. Pour into the prepared tin and bake in the centre of the oven for 40 minutes until a skewer comes out of the centre completely clean. Leave to cool on a wire rack in the tin.

Once the cake is cool, mix together the icing sugar, coconut and Malibu or lemon juice until glossy. Spoon the thick icing onto the top of the cake, smoothing with the back of the spoon as you go.

Turkish delight friendship cake

I made this for a very new friend who is a welcome tonic in my life. When pregnant she was addicted to all things flowery so I made her lavender shortbread and dainty violet creams. She even named her daughter Poppy. I am very lucky to be her Godmother.

This cake is light, easy to make and best of all, reminiscent of proper Turkish delight without the intense, concentrated sugar high. If the pistachios are threatening to blow the budget, leave them out. You can always use walnuts instead.

Serves 12

For the cake:
175g butter, softened,
    plus extra for greasing
175g caster sugar
3 large eggs, at room
    temperature, beaten
1 tsp vanilla extract
3 tbsp whole milk
175g self-raising flour
1 tsp baking powder
75g pistachios, roughly
    chopped

For the buttercream:
1 tsp rose water
1 tsp vanilla extract
10g honey
100g salted butter, softened
200g icing sugar
Pink gel food colouring
    (optional)
25g pistachios, roughly
    chopped

Grease and line a 22 x 18cm tin with baking paper. Preheat the oven to 170°C/gas mark 3 and place the shelf in the centre. To make the cake, cream the butter with the sugar until really light and creamy – this takes about 4 minutes in a stand mixer, 5 minutes with a handheld mixer or 10 minutes with a wooden spoon. Add the eggs gradually, dribble by dribble, mixing after each addition. Mix in the vanilla and milk. If the mixture curdles or looks grainy, add a tablespoon of flour to rebind the mixture.

Sift the flour and baking powder and then, in thirds, fold it into the butter mixture using a large metal spoon in a cutting motion. Gently fold in the pistachios. Pour the batter into your tin and bake for 35–40 minutes, or until golden on top and a skewer comes out clean. Leave to cool on a wire rack and remove from the tin as soon as it is cool enough to handle.

Make the buttercream. Beat the rose water, vanilla, honey and butter in a bowl until soft and creamy, using an electric mixer or a wooden spoon. Add a tablespoon of icing sugar at a time and beat after each addition until soft and fluffy. Add a dab of colouring if you are using it. Spread the buttercream over the cake and top with pistachios. Serve to friends, new and old.

Ideas for rose water

Add a teaspoon to lemonade or chilled Prosecco for a floral drink. Or add a drop to harissa to make a Middle Eastern marinade. Or a teaspoon in buttercream changes a simple Victoria sponge into something special. Or dot it onto light bulbs for the aroma of summer even in the darkest winter.

Pimms & lemonade cheesecake

I like to serve Pimms and lemonade at my parties whatever the time of year. It conjures memories of happy summer days. I like all the froufrou fruit and adornment. So here's a very easy cheesecake version, without any baking or gelatine soaking, and done in a few stages. Serve with... you guessed it.

Serves 12

For the base:
125g digestive biscuits
    (about 8), crushed
75g butter, melted
1 tbsp caster sugar

For the cheesecake:
350g cream cheese
85g icing sugar
Finely grated zest of 1 orange
Finely grated zest of 2 lemons
1 tbsp fresh orange juice
1 tbsp fresh lemon juice
300ml double cream, whipped

For the jelly:
150ml Pimms
135g block of full-sugar
    strawberry jelly (I use
    Hartleys), cut into cubes
A few mint leaves
A few strawberries,
    hulled and sliced

For the salad:
400g strawberries, hulled
    and quartered
1/3 cucumber, deseeded and
    chopped into 2cm chunks
150ml Pimms
1 tbsp finely chopped
    mint leaves

Start making this cheesecake the day before you need it.

Grease and line a 20cm springform tin (at least 7cm in height) with cling film – this will make it easier to remove later. Mix the biscuits, butter and sugar together and press into the tin using the back of a metal spoon. Chill in the fridge for 10 minutes.

To make the cheesecake layer, beat the cream cheese, icing sugar, both zests and juices in a stand mixer, with an electric handheld mixer or with a wooden spoon until combined. Gently fold through the whipped cream with a large metal spoon. Spoon onto your chilled base, smooth and refrigerate for 2 hours.

Make the jelly. Heat the Pimms in a small pan until it starts to bubble, then remove from the heat and add the jelly cubes. Stir until dissolved, pour into a jug and refrigerate. Arrange a few mint leaves and sliced strawberries on top of the cheesecake, then when the jelly has cooled and just started to set pour it over the cheesecake and place it back in the fridge for 2 hours until set firm. The jelly needs to have begun to set in the jug before pouring; if it is too liquid it will slip down the sides. If you leave it a little too long and the jelly won't level, simply use a hairdryer on a very low setting to 'melt' the jelly gently.

Mix all the salad ingredients and leave for an hour at room temperature to macerate. Carefully remove the cheesecake from the tin, unpeel the cling film and serve with the salad.

Ideas for a zestless lemon

Squeeze out the juice, measure, then add the same amount in grams of sugar – boil until the sugar dissolves and pour over cupcakes for mini drizzle cakes. Or squeeze over prawns and add chopped fresh chilli before frying over a high heat.

Summer's eve elderflower & gooseberry frangipane tart

I once tried to buy elderflowers from a garden centre and was informed that 'madam, elderflower is a weed, we do not sell weeds.' This slightly embarrassing situation highlighted my lack of green fingers but you know what, I reckon many the home cook would love to use fresh elderflowers. Fresh gooseberries are also hard to come by, so here we make life simple; delivering summer through tinned fruit and cordial.

Serves 12

For the pastry:

250g plain flour, plus extra
    for dusting
50g icing sugar
125g cold butter,
    cut into 1cm cubes
1 large egg, beaten

For the filling:

2 x 300g tins of gooseberries
    (drained weight 290g)
3 tbsp elderflower cordial
1 tbsp icing sugar

For the frangipane:

150g butter, softened
150g caster sugar
3 large eggs, at room
    temperature
150g ground almonds

For the icing:

25ml elderflower cordial
50g icing sugar

Make the pastry. Mix together the flour and icing sugar in a large bowl. Rub the butter into the flour mixture using clean hands, until you have a breadcrumb-like consistency. Add the egg and use a blunt knife to mix and pull the pastry together. Wrap in cling film and chill for 20 minutes.

Meanwhile, make the fruit filling by mashing the well-drained gooseberries with the elderflower cordial and icing sugar.

Preheat the oven to 180°C/gas mark 4. Make the frangipane. Beat the butter and sugar with a mixer or wooden spoon until light and creamy. Add the eggs a little at a time, beating well after each addition. Fold in the ground almonds and set aside.

Roll the pastry out on a floured surface to the thickness of a pound coin and about 24 x 24cm. Put both hands under the pastry, palm side up and fingers spread wide, and transfer to a 20cm loose-bottomed tart tin. Press into the corners and run the rolling pin over the top, cutting off any excess. Patch up any tears then pour in the filling, levelling with the back of a spoon. Spoon in the frangipane so it touches the edges, and bake in the middle of the oven for 35–40 minutes until the frangipane is brown and the pastry is crisp.

Leave to cool on a wire rack whilst in the tin. Once cool, remove from the tin, mix the cordial and sugar and drizzle over the top.

Ideas for ground almonds

Add a tablespoon to creamy curries for a taste reminiscent of korma. Or substitute pinenuts for almonds for a thrifty version of homemade pesto that's popular with kids.

Baking has held my hand through life — from childhood days stamping out pastry for jam tarts to student brownies baked in less than spotless kitchens. My 20s were stressful, it was all work and a lot of play, burning the candle at both ends and so I found solace in pie and biscuit making on rare weekend downtime. Ah, and then the Mummy years began and now baking is an assisted sport voted more fun than Play Doh in our house.

Baking isn't often necessary. You don't need to make treacle tart in order for the family to survive, so by the nature of it being a non-essential activity, it immediately denotes itself as a pleasure. An added extra to the normal daily menu, sprinkling joy wherever the results are shared. I try never to rush baking for fear that one day a hobby I love might become a chore.

Switching into baking mode begins with some music being carefully chosen, the switch and turn of the oven dial and the bubbling of the boiling kettle. Give me tea, a good recipe and some music to dance to whilst the treats bake and I'm a very happy woman.

Switching to Baking Mode

Leicestershire Stilton, caramelised onion & potato pie

This is my much praised pie (loved by Mr Hollywood) from my time on *The Great British Bake Off*. This is an 'assembly pie' as the work is in the pastry and the prepping. It's very good; you can feel the fatty goodness as you eat it. Don't let that put you off. Just enjoy it and eat salad tomorrow. Credit/debit. Metal dishes are always best for pies as they heat very quickly, meaning a crisper pastry. No soggy tops (or bottoms).

30g butter
280g onions (about 3 medium),
    peeled and thinly sliced
1 tsp salt, plus extra
    for cooking
2 tbsp caster sugar
930g potatoes (about
    10 medium), peeled and
    thinly sliced (I like Marabel)
140g crème fraîche
4 tbsp double cream
100g mature cheddar, grated
100g Stilton, crumbled
100g Gruyère, grated
Ground black pepper
1 tsp freshly grated nutmeg
500g pack of chilled puff pastry
Plain flour, for dusting
1 large egg, beaten

Ideas for nutmeg

Add a little grated nutmeg
to a myriad of dishes to really
bring out the flavour – biscuits,
béchamel sauce, pancakes,
parsnip soup, apple pie,
scones, fruitcake, carrot cake,
braised vegetables (especially
leeks)... the list goes on!
My best advice would be to
keep fresh nutmeg and a tiny
grater out with the salt and
pepper. It really is that useful.

Melt the butter in a pan and add the onions, salt and sugar.
Fry over a low heat, stirring occasionally, for 5–6 minutes
until lightly caramelised. Remove from the heat and set aside.
Cook the sliced potatoes in a large pan of boiling, salted water
for 8 minutes, drain well then set aside.

Mix the crème fraîche, cream and cheddar in a bowl. In another
bowl, mix the Stilton and Gruyère. Working in layers and from
the outside of the dish inwards (to achieve a domed effect),
add one quarter of the potatoes, a third of the onions and a third
of the Stilton mixture. My pie dish is 18cm wide on the bottom
and 24cm across the top. Sprinkle over a little pepper and the
nutmeg. Repeat the layers, seasoning as you go, then pour over
half the crème fraîche mixture. Repeat the layers, top with the
remaining crème fraîche and cover with the rest of the potato,
so the filling is not visible (preventing soggy pastry).

Preheat the oven to 200°C/gas mark 6. Roll the pastry out on
a well-floured work surface until it's about 5mm thick and square
in shape. It needs to be about 6cm wider than the edges of the
pie dish. Cut off two 1.5cm-wide strips from the sides of the
pastry. Brush the egg over the rim of the tin and fix the strips
onto it so that the rim is covered. Egg wash the strips.

Check that the pastry square is at least 2.5cm larger than
the tin all the way round by holding the tin above the pastry
and checking by eye. If large enough, put your hands under
the pastry, palm side up and fingers spread wide and lift gently
into the tin. Try not to stretch the pastry. Press the square
gently onto the pastry rim. Trim the pastry to about 5mm larger
than the edge of the pie tin using scissors. Dip your fork into
the flour and use it to seal and indent around the rim of the tin.
Keep re-flouring your fork to stop any dragging.

Take a blunt knife and 'knock up' the edges by fluffing up the
pastry of the rim and the lid until stuck together. This ensures
that they won't come apart during baking and there is a nice
thick-layered appearance. Egg wash the lid really well and cut
a cross in the top for steam to escape, creating a crisp and flaky
lid. Pop in the oven for 20 minutes, then turn the heat down to
180°C/gas mark 4. Bake for 1 hour. Serve with lots of green veg.

Falafel 'sausage' rolls

There's nothing piggy about these sausage rolls, they're as vegetarian as they come. They rely on one of my favourite take away treats, falafel. I first ate falafel at an ungodly hour on the streets of Utrecht. My friend and I had been looking for something to line our stomachs with and happened upon a kiosk selling falafel housed in soft pitta with crunchy slaw and chilli sauce. Here the falafel is encased in buttery puff pastry, though I still recommend a side of chilli sauce — maybe even some hummus too. Beware that three cloves of garlic is actually rather garlicky — so reduce if you prefer.

Makes 10

For the falafel:

397g tin of chickpeas
(drained weight 240g)
2 tbsp groundnut or
sunflower oil
1 small onion (about 60g),
peeled and finely chopped
3 garlic cloves, peeled
1 tsp ground cumin
1 tsp ground coriander
½ tsp dried chilli flakes
(optional)
Finely grated zest and
juice of 1 lemon
1 tbsp Greek yoghurt
1 tsp salt
1 tsp ground black pepper
60g frozen peas

For the assembly:

500g pack of chilled puff pastry
A little plain flour, for dusting
1 egg
A pinch of salt

Preheat the oven to 200°C/gas mark 6. Line a baking tray with non-stick greaseproof paper. Blend all the falafal ingredients except the peas using a stick blender or food processor until well blended but with a little texture still remaining. Add the frozen peas and mix through with a spoon.

Roll the puff pastry out onto a well-floured surface using a floured rolling pin to a thickness of a pound coin and into a 35 x 24cm rectangle. Cut the sheet of pastry in half lengthways so you have two long strips measuring 35 x 12cm then divide the filling between the two, fashioning it into a sausage shape along the middle of each strip of pastry. Beat the egg with a pinch of salt. Brush the egg wash along both long edges of each then pull the long edges up to meet in the middle, pinching firmly to secure. Lay both of the long sausage rolls on their side, with the pinched edges facing you, and cut each into 5 equal sausage rolls. Place on the baking tray, at least 3cm apart.

Brush every roll with plenty of egg wash and bake for 35–40 minutes until golden brown in colour and baked through. Eat warm or cold.

Man quiche

Imagine my surprise when after bagging my old-fashioned husband he revealed a penchant for quiche. My dad had always held firm that real men don't eat quiche. It turns out that very rarely dads can be wrong. This quiche is filling and meaty through the mushrooms but you can add a handful of fried lardons or chopped bacon. I promise the pastry recipe is easy but please don't feel guilty about buying it if you don't have the time.

For the pastry:

140g cold butter,
    cut into 1cm cubes
280g plain flour, plus extra
    for dusting
50g Parmesan or other hard
    cheese, finely grated
100ml very cold water (I keep
    a fresh bottle in the fridge
    for making pastry)

Or

500g pack of shortcrust pastry

For the filling:

140g leeks (about 1 large leek),
    chopped into rings
2 tbsp olive oil
30g butter
Pinch of salt
500g mushrooms, such
    as chestnut, sliced
1 tsp fresh thyme leaves
    or ½ tsp dried thyme
140g Gruyère or other hard
    cheese, grated
2 large eggs, lightly beaten
300ml double cream
Ground black pepper

If you are making your own pastry, rub the butter into the flour until you have a fine-breadcrumb consistency. Stir in the cheese and add the water, stirring with a blunt knife until it starts to come together. Use your hands to scoop it into a ball, without kneading. Wrap it in cling film and rest in the fridge.

Prepare the filling by very gently frying the leeks in the oil, butter and salt over a low heat. When just softened but not coloured, transfer to a dish then fry the mushrooms and thyme in the same pan in batches, frying for about 8 minutes, until any liquid released fries off. Mix the mushrooms, thyme, cheese, eggs, cream and pepper together, but keep the leeks separate. This is so the leeks don't sit on top and catch in the oven.

Roll the chilled pastry out on a lightly floured work surface using a rolling pin, into a circle that is 5cm larger in diameter than the tart tin (I use a 23cm loose-bottomed tart tin) and as thick as a pound coin. Transfer the pastry to the tin by gently placing both hands underneath it, spread wide with palms facing upwards. Push the pastry into the sides of the tin and run your rolling pin across the top to trim off the excess. Chill the pastry-lined tin for 15 minutes and preheat the oven to 200°C/gas mark 6. Bake the trimmings to nibble on while you wait. Waste not, want not!

Line the pastry with greaseproof paper and fill with baking beans, uncooked rice or dried beans. Bake for 15 minutes, remove the beans and paper, then bake for another 10 minutes. Remove the pastry case from the oven only when it looks entirely cooked through, then fill first with a layer of leeks, followed by the mushroom filling. Bake for 20–25 minutes until browned and a knife inserted in the centre shows no wet filling. I serve this with something honest and simple, like a green salad dressed with a little olive oil.

Ideas for fresh thyme

Chop, mix with lemon zest and use as a marinade-rub for pork. Or just freeze it on the stem and use the leaves direct from the freezer – they pull off really easily and are perfect for chucking into soups and over roasted vegetables.

Seeded granary rolls

My childhood memories of convenience-led comfort food come back to haunt me as adult guilty indulgences. Some days I love a bowl of piping hot alphabet spaghetti with lots of strong cheddar grated over the top. Or a bowl of steaming hot sweet and thick tomato soup. For me, both of these edible comfort blankets are best with a crusty seeded roll spread with salted butter. These freeze incredibly well so make a batch and freeze as lone soldiers, ready for when in need of comfort.

Makes 12

250g granary flour, plus extra for dusting
250g strong wholemeal spelt flour
1 tsp fast action dried yeast
1¼ tsp salt
1 tsp caster sugar
1 tbsp groundnut oil, plus extra for greasing
350ml lukewarm water
75g butter, softened
60g mixed seeds
30g oats
1 egg

Mix both types of flour with the yeast, 1 teaspoon of the salt, the sugar, oil and water in a large bowl using a metal spoon. Set aside for 10 minutes. Knead the dough on an oiled work surface (see page 133 for instructions) then leave to prove in a large bowl covered in cling film. Don't worry if the dough looks too wet, it is meant to be – just keep your hands well-oiled and remember, with bread dough, the wetter the better!

When the dough has doubled in size (this is dependent on the warmth of the room, the warmer it is the quicker it will be) and a finger pushed into the dough by about 2cm pings back up and leaves only a slightly depressed mark, it's ready to knock back. Push the dough down and flip it over, then add the butter, seeds, and all but 1 tablespoon of the oats and massage into the dough. It might feel like the butter won't absorb at first as it will slide about the surface, but keep going. It will.

Roll the dough out on an oiled surface into a thick sausage shape. Cut into thirds using a serrated knife, then cut each third into 4 equal pieces so you have 12 lumps in all. Sprinkle some flour onto a large baking tray. Flatten each piece of dough in your palm. Take the edges of the dough and fold into the centre until you have a smaller sphere. Turn it over and put the folded, slightly pinched looking end down on the baking tray so they are 3cm apart. Sprinkle over some flour and cover loosely with cling film. Leave the rolls to double in size; in a hot kitchen this takes about 30 minutes, in a cold one as long as 2 hours. Don't worry if the rolls spread and look flat; this is due to using spelt flour and does not affect the taste.

Preheat the oven to 200°C/gas mark 6. Beat the egg with the remaining salt and brush each of the rolls with the egg wash. Scatter over the remaining oats. Top with egg wash to help them stick and slash a 1cm-deep cut into the tops. I use a very sharp serrated knife for this. Bake for 10–15 minutes until the rolls are well browned and can easily be removed from the tray. They should sound hollow when you tap them underneath. Place on a wire rack to cool.

Stilton and walnut bread rolls

Tastes change over time. My mother tells me I gobbled up liver casserole and tongue sandwiches as a child with aplomb. They are now my least favourite foods. My love of blue cheese has grown from a vehement dislike as a child to a near addiction these days. If it isn't your thing try white Stilton instead.

300ml water
500g strong white flour,
    plus extra for dusting
7g fast action dried yeast
2 tsp salt
1 tsp caster sugar
30ml walnut or olive oil,
    plus extra for greasing
150g Stilton, crumbled
150g walnuts, finely chopped
1 egg
A pinch of salt

Boil 100ml of the water in a small pan, then mix with 200ml of cold water from the tap. In a large bowl, mix together the flour, yeast, salt, sugar, oil and all the water and give it a good stir with a large spoon. Oil your work surface and hands, then tip the shaggy dough out onto the work surface and start kneading.

Everyone kneads differently. Some pick the dough up and slap it back onto the table. Others stretch it from the centre up to the 2nd hand on a clock, pulling it back down to the centre, turning it 90 degrees and repeating. Others use the dough hook on a stand mixer. Whatever method you use knead it until smooth and elastic looking. To test if it is ready, take a piece the size of a plum and stretch it between your two thumbs and two index fingers until you can almost see though it. If it stretches easily then the gluten has developed; if it breaks then keep kneading.

Place the dough back in the bowl, cover with cling film and leave to prove. This will depend on the warmth of the room – the hotter the room the quicker it will be. When the dough has doubled and a finger pushed to the depth of about 2cm leaves a mark but pops back a little, it's ready to knock back. Push the dough down and flip it over, then add the Stilton and walnuts, folding it again and again until evenly distributed.

Sprinkle flour onto a large baking tray. Roll the dough out on an oiled surface into a thick sausage shape. Use a serrated knife to cut the dough into eight equal pieces. Take each piece and flatten it in your palm. Then take the edges of the dough and fold into the centre until you have a smaller sphere of dough. Turn it over and put the folded, slightly pinched looking end down on the baking tray, spacing them 3cm apart. Sprinkle flour over the top and cover loosely with cling film to prove again.

Preheat the oven to 220°C/gas mark 7. When the rolls have doubled, about 30 minutes in a hot kitchen and 2 hours in a cold one, beat together the egg and salt and brush over the rolls. Cut a 1cm-deep slash into the tops using a sharp serrated knife.

Bake for 10–15 minutes until the rolls are well browned and can easily be lifted from the tray albeit in a grid of baked together rolls. They should sound hollow when you tap them underneath. Place on a wire rack to cool.

Orange, fig and sultana flapjacks

The sunny warmth of orange zest combined with dried figs makes me dream of a childhood holiday spent walking through Tunisian orange groves and riding on humpy bumpy camels. Like all flapjacks these are easy peasy and no one could possibly feel sad when chowing down on one of these energy-giving squares.

Makes 12

250g salted butter, plus extra
  for greasing
225g soft dark brown sugar
150g golden syrup
Finely grated zest of 1 orange
500g rolled oats
100g dried figs, chopped
150g sultanas

Preheat the oven to 180°C/gas mark 4 and grease and line a 25 x 20cm tin. Melt the butter, sugar, syrup and orange zest in a large saucepan over a medium heat. The aim is to dissolve all the ingredients so that they are smooth, but to not lose any volume through boiling so be careful not to overheat. Add the oats, figs and sultanas and stir well until evenly coated. Tip into the prepared tin and use a piece of greaseproof paper to flatten the top and make sure the flapjack is evenly distributed in the tin. Bake for 40 minutes until the edges start to brown. Whilst still warm in the tin, score into 12 squares. Allow to cool completely before cutting along the score lines.

Ideas for zestless orange

Squeeze the juice and simply drink it straight up – or mix with another fresh juice like mango or apple for a breakfast vitamin C hit. Or squeeze, measure the juice in millilitres and add the same amount in grams of caster sugar, then heat in a pan until the sugar dissolves and use while still warm to drizzle over freshly baked cupcakes for easy sticky orange drizzles. Or simply use as a marinade for chicken breasts along with a little soy, freshly grated ginger and honey, and bake in a preheated oven at 180°C/gas mark 4 for 30 minutes until the juices run clear.

St Clements breakfast swirls

Anything baked in a spiral seems inherently happy to me, coiled up and sprung, ready to ping into action. I love this strategy for introducing flavour to breads as it feels somehow restrained. Not a simple case of throwing the herbs or spices into the dough, instead a flavour-present carefully wrapped up and in, though still on display. No huge surprises. St Clements too is a sunny flavour, hopeful for sunny lemonade days. These are brushed with a marmalade glaze, making these breakfast buns popular with men, who do seem to be more partial to marmalade than girls, I've noticed.

Makes 12

For the dough:

80ml whole or semi-
   skimmed milk
7g fast action dried yeast
2 tbsp caster sugar
230g strong white flour,
   plus extra for dusting
½ tsp salt
1 large egg
30g salted butter, melted
   and left to cool slightly

For the filling and glaze:

60g granulated brown sugar
Finely grated zest of 2 lemons
Finely grated zest of 2 oranges
15g salted butter, melted
3 tbsp marmalade, warmed and
   strained to remove any shred

Warm the milk to about body temperature, heating it in the microwave in short bursts. Mix together the yeast, caster sugar, flour and salt, then stir in the egg, melted butter and warmed milk. Stir well then knead (see page 133 for instructions on kneading) until smooth and elastic. Leave in a bowl covered with cling film until doubled in size – this can take anything from 40 minutes to 2 hours depending on how warm the room is. The hotter the kitchen, the faster the rise.

Line a 30 x 26cm roasting tray with non-stick greaseproof paper. Knock the dough back with your hands to deflate. On a floured surface and using a floured rolling pin, roll the dough into a rectangle shape measuring about 23 x 32cm. In a small bowl, mix the brown sugar with both zests. Brush the dough rectangle with the melted butter then evenly sprinkle over the brown sugar mixture. Roll the dough up, starting from the long edge, like a swiss roll. Cut along the length into 12 equal pieces. Place each swirl in the roasting tray, about 2cm apart, and cover loosely with cling film – this way they will just touch once they've proved, so you can tear the rolls apart after baking as if from an artisan bakery.

Preheat the oven to 190°C/gas mark 5. Once the rolls have doubled in size, bake for about 10 minutes until well risen and browned. Remove from the tin using the paper and place on a wire rack. Brush with the marmalade and leave to cool.

Syrupy vanilla muffins

Thomas Land is a regular haunt of the Bell family. No princesses and ballet lessons for me. It's all about trains and knights in this house. The first time we visited the train wonder that is Thomas Land, we'd only been on site for half an hour and I was already plotting how to convert my day pass to a season ticket, such is the train love in our family. The boys pester to ride Thomas, Diesel and Jeremy. I pester for the syrupy muffins in the café located by the zoo. So often I buy a muffin and am disappointed at their dry and often tasteless state. Not at Thomas Land, which should be renamed Land of Syrupy Muffins as far as I'm concerned.

Makes 12

50g dark muscovado sugar
65g caster sugar
115g salted butter
230g golden syrup, plus an extra 60g for drizzling
2 tbsp custard powder
210g self-raising flour
150ml whole or semi-skimmed milk
1 large egg, at room temperature

Preheat the oven to 160°C/gas mark 3 and line a 12-hole muffin tray with cases. Melt the sugars, butter and the 230g of syrup in a large saucepan over a low heat until everything has dissolved. Remove the pan from the heat and leave to cool slightly.

Use a wooden spoon to beat the custard powder and flour into the melted sugar mixture, then beat in the milk. Beat in the egg until the mixture is smooth and well combined – it should be very runny. Pour the mixture into the muffin cases (using a jug if it is easier) until half to three-quarters filled. Bake for about 45 minutes until they're golden and a skewer comes out of the centre of the muffin clean.

Whilst the muffins are still warm spoon 1 teaspoon of golden syrup over the top of each. Remove from the tray and leave to cool on a wire rack.

My best high-hat scones

I think the sign of a good scone is when it's towering so high you worry for its safety. It should teeter on the edge of lofty ridiculousness and split happily, as if relieved those topple verging days are over. Scones freeze like a dream so if you don't get through them all on the day of baking conserve them in the freezer. Whatever you do don't keep them in a tin and expect them to taste wonderful the next day. They won't. Scones like to be gobbled up. With clotted cream and jam if you're game.

Makes 5-6

300g plain flour, plus extra for dusting
15g baking powder
90g very cold salted butter, cut into 1cm cubes
145ml very cold whole or semi-skimmed milk, plus extra for brushing

Mix the flour and baking powder together until well combined. Stir the very cold butter pieces through the flour with a blunt knife until all the pieces are well coated. Wash your hands in cold water and rub the fat into the flour. You can also use a pastry cutter for this job if you have one.

When you have a breadcrumb-like consistency, pour the milk over the butter and flour mixture and bring together with a blunt knife, then use your hands to pull it together by squeezing gently. Wrap in cling film and pop in the fridge for 30 minutes.

Preheat the oven to 220°C/gas mark 7 and check the rack is at the top of the oven. Cover a baking sheet with non-stick greaseproof paper. Flour your work surface, then pop the scone dough onto it. Roll to about a 3cm thickness then use a 6cm scone cutter dipped in flour to cut straight down, without twisting or turning it. Place on a baking sheet and repeat until all the dough is used; you can re-squidge it but the scones won't be as tender. Brush the tops of the scones with a little milk, making sure that none of it runs down the sides as it will stop a good rise. Bake immediately for 10–15 minutes until the tops are golden brown and the scones are well risen. A good scone has a little split around the middle, ready for breaking in two with your hands. Knives only required for the jam and cream.

Peasant's pretzel brownies

I call these peasant's brownies for they contain not a smidgen of melted chocolate. Over the years I have made many a brownie recipe and my bugbear has always been just how much good-quality chocolate has to be sacrificed to the cause. Brownies should, in my book, be a regular treat, not a seldom-made costly exercise. These brownies manage to substitute cocoa for fine chocolate and with no ill effect. They're just as squidgy and moreish and very rich. And the crunchy salty pretzels are decidedly good with the sweet fudgey chocolate ooze, but you can leave them out if salt and sweet isn't your thing.

Makes 16 small rich bites

70g salted butter, plus
    extra for greasing
200g caster sugar
100ml vegetable or
    groundnut oil
45g cocoa powder
65g self-raising flour
¼ tsp salt
¼ tsp baking powder
2 large eggs, at room
    temperature
1 tsp vanilla extract
16 salted pretzels (optional)

Preheat the oven to 180°C/gas mark 4. Grease and line a 20cm square baking tin. Gently heat the butter, sugar and oil in a medium saucepan, until the butter has melted but the sugar is still a little gritty. Add all the ingredients except for the pretzels to the saucepan and stir until combined. Pour the batter into the prepared tin. If using the pretzels, gently place them over the top of the batter in a grid pattern so that they will be easy to cut up.

Bake for 20–25 minutes on the middle shelf of the oven, until the top of the brownie has set but there's still a little bit of movement when you shake the tin. You do not want an overcooked brownie. Remove from the oven and allow to cool in the tin, then cut into squares. Wrap well if you're not eating these immediately, to maintain the all-important goo-factor.

Momma's Cornish ginger fairings

I was very close to my grandmother, named Momma (pronounced 'Mom-mar') by my toddler self. She was about 5 foot nothing, obsessed with her 'bloody hair' as she called it and loved nothing more than taking me for an underage afternoon glass of wine at the only French bistro in Leicester. She was a thoroughly bad influence and I adored her for it. She loved food but hated cooking, and saw it as unnecessary drudgery. Imagine my surprise after she died to find a well-worn recipe book in her house with this handwritten into it. Not once did she make these for me and yet they are wonderful! Here's the recipe translated into metric.

Makes about 15

115g butter
1 tbsp golden syrup
170g self-raising flour
85g caster sugar
1 tsp ground ginger, or more if you like a strong ginger taste
½ tsp bicarbonate of soda

Preheat the oven to 190°C/gas mark 5 and line 2 baking trays with non-stick greaseproof paper. Melt the butter and syrup in a saucepan over a low heat until dissolved. Add the flour, sugar, ginger and bicarbonate of soda and give it a good mix with a wooden spoon. Leave the mixture to cool for a few minutes as you will need to be able to handle it.

Using your hands, form handfuls of the warm mixture into balls about 4cm across; you should make about 15. Place them on the lined trays, making sure that there's plenty of space for them to spread in the oven. I leave a 5cm gap between each.

Bake in the oven for 12–15 minutes until the dough has spread into cracked looking biscuits. If you like your biscuits with a bit of 'chew' (more cookie-like) then take them out when only the sides are brown. If you like them crunchy then let the whole biscuit get a suntan. Let them cool on the baking tray for a few minutes then transfer to a wire rack to cool completely.

Sunken blackcurrant squash love cupcakes

My mum didn't do can't-haves; she fed me well and allowed me treats. I think it worked in that I don't lie awake at night wishing to gorge myself on leftover cake and roast potatoes. However, there was one thing that was off limits – Ribena. And of course that meant I loved it with a passion. I buy the sugar-free version for drinking, but the full version for baking. These cupcakes use polenta, a gritty baking addition that makes you think you're eating something very sugary. If you like lemon then add a little zest to the batter, as the crunch of polenta and the zing of lemon are natural bedfellows.

Makes 12

115g salted butter, softened
200g caster sugar
2 large eggs, at room
    temperature, beaten
70g fine polenta
125g self-raising flour
1 tsp baking powder
1 tsp custard powder
85g dried cherries and berries
275g icing sugar
40ml blackcurrant squash
    (I use Ribena)
12 heart-shaped sweets

Ideas for polenta

Serve polenta in place of mash – with lots of Parmesan and finely chopped rosemary stirred through, sausages on the side and a poached egg on top. Or add crushed garlic and leave to cool and set in a lined tin, then cut into fingers, brush with melted butter, grill and serve with chargrilled peppers, onions and courgettes.

Preheat the oven to 180°C/gas mark 4 and line a 12-hole cupcake tray with cases. Beat together the butter and caster sugar until very light and fluffy; this will take about 5 minutes with a mixer or double that time using a wooden spoon. Dribble in the eggs about a tablespoon at a time, beating well after each addition until they are all incorporated. Sift the polenta, flour, baking powder and custard powder into the creamed mixture and fold it together with a large metal spoon, using slicing motions so as not to knock the air out of all the ingredients. Don't worry if you do knock a lot of the air out, however – it will just mean you'll end up with slightly dipped cupcakes, which will mean you will just have to use more icing.

Pop 1 tablespoon of mixture into each case, sprinkle with a few dried cherries and berries and top with another tablespoon of the mixture. Repeat until all the cases are full then bake for 20 minutes until well-risen, golden brown and a toothpick comes out of the centre of the cupcakes clean. Remove them from the tray and leave to cool on a wire rack.

Mix the icing sugar and squash together until very stiff and spoon over the cooled cakes. Add a sweet to the top of each and allow to set before eating.

Toe-warming whisky sour treacle tart

Names can be misleading. There's no brandy in a snap, nothing canine about a hot dog (you hope), no toad in the hole. And no treacle in a treacle tart. I prefer it with the sweeter golden syrup. I also prefer it with a dram of whisky.

This is the most well-behaved pastry I know. I'd urge you to have a go with this recipe as it really is easy as pie... or rather tart. Of course shop-bought stuff is a fine substitute if you'd rather not. As for leftover scraps, roll them out, stamp into some shapes and bake as little pastry biscuits to be enjoyed with a cup of tea.

Serves 12

250g plain flour, plus extra
   for dusting
50g icing sugar
125g cold butter, cut into
   2cm cubes
1 large egg, beaten
Finely grated zest and juice
   of 1 lemon
150g fresh breadcrumbs
400g golden syrup
10ml whisky

Ideas for a juiceless, zestless lemon

Waste not, want not – stuff into a whole chicken along with an onion and a couple of uncrushed garlic cloves, massage a little olive oil into the skin and roast in the oven at 180°C/gas mark 4, time dependent on weight. Or add to boiling water and drink as a breakfast cleanser after one too many whisky nightcaps.

Mix together the flour and icing sugar. Use your hands to rub the butter into the flour until it looks like very fine breadcrumbs. Using a blunt knife to mix, bind the mixture with the egg. Pull the pastry together, wrap in cling film and refrigerate for 1 hour.

Meanwhile, mix the zest with the breadcrumbs and set aside. Pour the golden syrup into a saucepan, add the lemon juice and the whisky then gently heat for a couple of minutes until the syrup has loosened and everything is well combined. Add the zesty breadcrumbs and stir well. Take off the heat and set aside to cool. Preheat the oven to 180°C/gas mark 4 about 15 minutes before the pastry has finished resting.

Roll the pastry out on a floured surface, working in one direction only (don't roll backwards and forwards, this makes for tough pastry), picking it up and turning it after each few rolls to ensure you end up with a rough circle shape about 3mm-thick and slightly larger than the tart tin. Pick it up by placing both hands flattened, fingers apart and palm side up, under the pastry circle and lift it into a 24cm tart tin then push it gently into the sides.

Run a rolling pin over the top to remove any excess pastry. Line with a piece of baking paper and fill with baking beans, uncooked rice or pulses and bake for 10 minutes. When the edges are starting to very lightly brown, remove the paper and beans and bake for 2 minutes to ensure the bottom is completely crisp. Remove from the oven, spoon in the filling and level with the back of a spoon. If you want, you can decorate the top with anything you fancy made from the leftover pastry. Bake for another 15–20 minutes. I like to eat this hot with clotted cream ice cream but it's also very good with custard.

Hex family stollen

Otherwise known as Weihnacht Stollen. Our pal Big Stu is half Dutch Indonesian and this is the gift his mother bestows on all her nearest and dearest in the run up to Christmas. In our house it is the law to eat this for breakfast, grilled, for the week leading up to the big day, sometimes with rum butter. A huge thanks to Wanda Hex for sharing this wonderful recipe and hopefully not being too upset that I have meddled with it a little to make it easier for us mere mortals.

Makes 1 stollen

For the dough:

375g strong white flour,
   plus extra for dusting
7g salt
75g salted butter, melted,
   plus extra for greasing
170ml lukewarm whole or
   semi-skimmed milk
140g caster sugar
14g fast action dried yeast
1 egg yolk
150g dried mixed fruit
50g mixed peel
300g marzipan

To decorate:

25g butter, melted
4 tbsp icing sugar
25g flaked almonds, toasted

Place the flour in a large bowl and make a hole in the middle. Sprinkle the salt around the edges, then add the butter, milk, 100g of the sugar and the yeast to the well and mix slowly, drawing more flour into the middle. Once well mixed, add the egg yolk and keep mixing until a dough forms. Knead for 10 minutes (see technique on page 133) until smooth and elastic. Return to the bowl, cover with cling film and leave to prove.

When doubled in size (the cooler it is, the longer it will take) tip it onto the work surface and knead in the dried fruit and peel. Return to the bowl, cover and rest for 10 minutes.

Roll the dough on a floured surface to an oblong about 34 x 24 x 1cm. Roll the marzipan into a 24cm-long sausage and place in the middle in line with the long edge of dough. Fold one of the long edges over the marzipan and press down to wrap it tightly in dough. There will be a small lip of dough sticking out.

Place on a greased baking sheet, cover loosely with cling film and leave to double in size. This is an enriched dough so the rising will be slow. Just before baking dust lightly with flour to stop the surface of dried fruit from burning.

Preheat the oven to 200°C/gas mark 6 and bake for 30–35 minutes until really brown. Brush away any fruit that's a little burnt and place on a wire rack with old newspaper underneath. While it is still hot, brush with the melted butter, sieve over half the icing sugar, add the almonds and sprinkle with the rest of the sugar. Leave to cool. Wrap and keep for at least a week (preferably 2) before cutting; this allows the flavours to develop.

My mum's classic 1970s coffee & walnut cake

My mum has a theory that she's not a great cake baker. I beg to differ as her coffee and walnut is the stuff of dreams; pillowy soft sponge with just the right amount of bitter coffee and almost buttery walnuts. A huge slice and a cup of strong black coffee is my pick-me-up heaven.

Serves 10-12

For the cake:
170g baking margarine or
    softened butter
170g caster sugar
3 large eggs, at room
    temperature, beaten
2 tbsp strong black coffee,
    cooled (if you have a fancy
    coffee machine or a cafe
    nearby then use espresso,
    otherwise use instant)
200g self-raising flour
60g walnuts, chopped

For the icing and decoration:
170g salted butter, softened
450g icing sugar
1 tbsp strong black coffee
110g walnuts halves,
    or less if you prefer

Preheat the oven to 180°C/gas mark 4 and grease and line two 20cm round, non-stick cake tins with baking paper. Cream together the margarine or butter and the caster sugar until light and fluffy. This will take about 4 minutes using a mixer or about 7–8 minutes using a wooden spoon and some elbow grease.

Slowly add the eggs a little at a time and beat well after each addition – this does take a little time but is worth it for a superior texture. If it curdles, just add a tablespoon of flour to rebind the mixture and carry on mixing as before. Beat in the coffee.

Sift the flour and fold into the mixture using a large metal spoon in a smooth slicing motion, being gentle so that the air is not beaten out. Fold in the walnuts. Split the batter equally between the tins and level with a knife. Bake in the middle of the oven for about 35 minutes but do check after 25 if your oven is over zealous. The cake is ready when the edges have slightly shrunk away from the sides and a toothpick comes out of the centre of the cake clean. Leave to cool a little in the tin, then remove and let cool on a wire rack.

Meanwhile, make the icing. Cream the butter until pale and fluffy using a mixer or a wooden spoon. Add the icing sugar a tablespoonful at a time, beating well after each addition. Add the coffee and beat well. For a mousse-like icing flecked with air I beat at the highest setting for 7 minutes in my stand mixer. Sandwich the cakes together using half of the buttercream, then spread the rest over the top and decorate with walnuts.

So many of life's conundrums are answered with common sense. A few years ago, I found myself making batch after batch of macarons in preparation for biscuit week in *The Great British Bake Off*, and becoming increasingly more upset and incredulous that they kept flopping into sunken little blobs. One evening, my husband walked into the kitchen to find me shedding tears over them. Ridiculous, yes, but it's the wisdom he imparted that's more important – he simply suggested I change the recipe… for repeating the same action and expecting different results is the definition of madness.

He was right of course, and so I come to think of children who range from being a little reticent with new food to downright fearful. What to do with them? Certainly don't engage in repetitive battles at teatime. Who has the time or inclination for that? I say get them in the kitchen, with their own knife, chopping board and apron, then set about preparing dinner. They may not eat the first few meals they prepare but give it a week or so of different meal experiments and as their cooking skills grow so too will their palate.

Recipes for Chefs in the Making

Vegan peach & pecan smoothie muffins

These were made with the boys when a vegan friend was coming for dinner. I had low expectations; such is my dairy addiction when baking. And yet they were light and sweet and delicious. Perfect served warm with vegan ice cream or cold as a treat with a cup of tea. They're low maintenance, as they don't mind being beaten well in some places and little in others. These have become a staple in our house.

190g plain flour
135g caster sugar
2 tsp baking powder
½ tsp bicarbonate of soda
½ tsp salt
70g pecans, roughly chopped
410g tin of peach slices
   (drained weight 340g) or
   3 fresh peaches, stones
   and skin removed
80ml vegetable oil
1 tsp vanilla extract

Preheat the oven to 180°C/gas mark 4 and fill a 12-hole muffin tin with cases. In a large mixing bowl, mix together the flour, sugar, baking powder, bicarbonate of soda, salt and pecans. In a separate bowl, whizz the peach slices, oil and vanilla together with a handheld mixer until smooth. Stir the peach mixture into the dry ingredients until combined.

Spoon into the cases equally until just over half full and bake for 25–30 minutes until risen, brown, and a toothpick comes out of the middle of the muffins clean. Remove from the tin and leave to cool on a wire rack.

Mix it up breakfast muffins

Muffins are undoubtedly one of the easiest things to make with children; a long attention span is not necessary and they're happy to be haphazardly mixed. In fact they're all the better for it as no one wants an overworked muffin. These freeze well so you really don't need to gobble all 12 of them immediately, just freeze on the day of baking and leave out to defrost before you go to bed. And for adults I'd fully advise adding a sprinkling of fiery crushed chillies.

Makes 12

2 large eggs, at room temperature
80g vegetable oil
190ml whole or semi-skimmed milk
40g Greek yoghurt
100g wholemeal self-raising flour
175g white self-raising flour
10g baking powder
1 tsp cayenne pepper
80g pitted black olives, halved
200g feta cheese, cut into 1cm cubes
4 spring onions, finely chopped
20g oats

Preheat the oven to 190°C/gas mark 5 and line a 12-hole muffin tin with cases. Use a wooden spoon to mix together the eggs, oil, milk and yoghurt. In a separate bowl mix the flours, baking powder, cayenne pepper, olives, cheese and spring onion until all the ingredients are well covered in flour, then pour the wet mixture over the top and stir until just combined, but no more.

Fill the cases equally, until almost full; sprinkle a few oats over the top of each muffin and bake for 25–30 minutes until well risen and lightly brown. Remove from the tin and leave to cool on a wire rack and eat for breakfast, warm or cold.

'Easy as' cheese biscuits

These were a favourite afternoon baking activity when I first had my youngest son Max. Older brother Charlie (a whopping two and a half at the time) and I would race to bake against what we called the crying-clock. Max's tolerance for any activity not involving me holding him and singing the 'We love you Maxi' song was about 10 minutes.

These biscuits, I am pleased to report, can be made in ten minutes flat — and that's with a toddler helper. Better still, the recipe can be memorised, albeit in imperial measures — easy as 1, 2, 3. Even better, they're baked in only 10 more minutes.

Makes about 12

2oz cold butter,
   cut into 1cm cubes
3oz plain flour, plus extra
   for dusting
1oz Parmesan or other
   hard cheese, grated
1 large egg

Preheat the oven to 180°C/gas mark 4. Line a baking sheet with baking paper. Using your fingertips, rub the butter into the flour until you have a breadcrumb-like consistency. Add the cheese and stir with a wooden spoon. Make a well in the centre of the dry mixture, crack the egg into it and mix well until you have a very sticky, doughy mess.

Flour your work surface well and spoon the dough onto it. Cover the sticky dough with lots more flour — for once this isn't a recipe where you have to urge children to be conservative with flour dredging. Flatten with your palm until about 5mm thick, then cut out shapes with cutters that have been dipped in flour and pop onto the baking sheet. This dough happily re-rolls so squidge together any leftovers and pat down again.

Bake for about 10 minutes until they look a bit bubbly. Remove from the oven and let sit on the tray for 2 minutes before transferring to a wire rack to cool. Eat in front of children's TV with a beaker of juice or, possibly even better, after 7pm with a hunk of cheese, a few olives and a vat of red wine.

These biscuits, coming from a wet dough, go stale quickly — so eat on the day of baking or re-crisp in the oven the day after.

Banish the breadsticks grissini

We all make decisions on what we will and won't buy in. Me? I rarely buy pudding but there's always a jar of pesto in the fridge and one of those giant tubs of green Thai curry paste bought from the supermarket. They're my shortcuts. As for breadsticks, well I do buy them, but I endeavour to make them, as the bought ones are just so dry and easy to shatter. These grissini are enough to make me banish the breadsticks forever.

Makes 27

500g strong white flour
7g fast action dried yeast
10g salt
35ml olive oil, plus extra
   for greasing
270ml warm water

Line 2 baking trays with non-stick greaseproof paper. Mix all the ingredients together with a spoon then knead (see page 133) until smooth and elastic. I give each child some dough to work on, as smaller amounts seem less daunting. Leave to prove in a bowl covered in cling film until doubled in size (the time this takes is dependent on the warmth of the room – the hotter it is the faster the dough will rise) then ask the children to punch it down with well-oiled hands. Snip off 30g pieces and roll out on a well-oiled surface into long sausage shapes about 1cm wide and 30cm long. They need to be quite thin because they need to prove again and will grow another centimetre or so.

Place the sticks of dough on the lined baking trays and cover with some very loose cling film or an upturned deep roasting tin, allowing room for the dough to prove and rise. Preheat the oven to 220°C/gas mark 7. When double the size (again the time will depend on the warmth of the room) bake for 8–10 minutes until browned and baked through. Cool on a wire rack. These keep for a week in a tin.

Cut-out sandwiches

I can hear scoffing from many a parent at the sheer ridiculousness and wastefulness of making sandwiches in the shape of bears/trains/stars etc. I know that children need to be able to eat food in a regular, adult, normal format. So this isn't a 'recipe' to be repeated every day. I just think children should be allowed to enjoy and revel in their childlike ways every now and again. Before they start rolling their eyes and slamming doors and losing their sticky out tummies.

These are the fillings and shapes that we sometimes indulge in after a particularly fraught morning. Cut-out sandwiches soothe many a highly-strung child and parent.

Butter, softened
Sliced white bread (the cheap stuff is best)
Filling of your choice – our favourites are grated red Leicester cheese, hummus mixed with grated carrot, Marmite, ham and cheese, egg mayonnaise and cold cooked sausage

If necessary, use a very short blitz in the microwave to soften the butter, as manufactured white bread won't withstand any overzealous buttering with hard fat. Cut out as many shapes, in pairs, from the bread as you can muster with cookie cutters or special sandwich cutters. I hate waste, so pop the remnants into a plastic bag, freeze and use for feeding the ducks.

Match pairs of the shape and butter the inside of the slices. I'd suggest you do this job and leave the cutting of the shapes to the helper(s), working in production-line fashion. Take each pair and add your chosen sandwich filling. These sandwiches will need a little squeeze to keep them together as they don't have crusts to do this job.

Eat in front of the TV for a special lunch. If it's a really special lunch then jam and/or chocolate spread might be permissible as a filling. If it really is one of those days eat with crisps that look like bacon rashers.

Scrunch-it-up apricot & pistachio stuffing balls

These got their name one Christmas morning when my eldest son asked how you make a stuffing ball. Slightly preoccupied with basting, chopping and trying to locate the hidden goose fat I hurriedly replied 'you just scrunch them up' which really, is the exact instruction to follow. There's a lot of leaf removal for this recipe, perfect for kids who perpetually ask what they can do to help.

Makes 8–9

50g dried apricots
30g pistachios
1 small onion, peeled and
    finely chopped
A little olive oil
70g breadcrumbs
1 tsp dried sage
3 sprigs of fresh thyme
1 large egg, beaten

Depending on the age of the child, either chop the apricots with scissors and the pistachios with a knife for them or let them do it under supervision. I use the onion raw, but if you prefer a less pungent taste, gently fry the onion in oil for about 4 minutes until softened. Let cool completely before adding to the mixture.

Preheat the oven to 180°C/gas mark 4. Line a baking tray with greaseproof paper. Tip the breadcrumbs into a large bowl and add the apricots, pistachios, sage and onion. Pick the thyme leaves off their stalks and add the leaves to the mixture. Give it a really good mix then add the egg and scrunch it all up with clean hands to bind. Taking a tablespoon of mixture at a time, scrunch between your hands and place them on the baking trays leaving a 3cm space between each.

Bake for 15–20 minutes until golden brown and cooked through. If you are serving this with roast meat, bake them whilst your meat is resting. Serve with your roast or even just as a snack.

Sandwich bake

A savoury bread and butter style pudding using regular sandwiches instead of slices of buttered bread. This is great for little ones practising their sandwich-making skills. It won't matter if the knife goes though the bread, in fact it makes for a better bake. Try to resist helping too much – sometimes you need to mangle a few pieces of bread to learn the hard way.

Serves 2 adults and 2 small children with salad or beans

20g butter, softened, plus extra for greasing
4 slices of white bread
70g cheese, grated
2 slices of ham
250ml semi-skimmed or whole milk
1 large egg
Ground black pepper (optional)

Grease a 24 x 14cm, 4cm deep ovenproof dish with a little butter. Butter one side of all the bread and make into sandwiches by scattering 2 of the slices with a third of the cheese each and cover with a slice of ham. Place the other two slices on top and squash together a little. Using scissors, cut each sandwich into four triangles, then line up in the dish with the point of the triangle facing upwards.

Use a fork to beat together the milk, egg and a little pepper then pour over the sandwiches to cover. Leave to soak for 10 minutes. Meanwhile, preheat the oven to 190°C/gas mark 5. Sprinkle the remaining cheese over the top and bake for 35 minutes until set and brown. Serve with baked beans for a TV dinner, kid style.

Baa Baa's veggie paella

Baa Baa is my dad. Much as he has tried to get the boys to call him Grandpa they persist in this baby name they conjured back when 'P's caused much trouble and strife. My dad makes this to use up any veggies on the verge of being sacrificed to the compost heap. It is a great way to get little ones preparing vegetables and there's no raw meat to stress out the food hygiene inspector in all parents. This doesn't for a second even pretend to moonlight as a proper paella. Can be eaten cold as a rice salad the next day.

Serves 2 children

½ red pepper
3 tomatoes
30g frozen peas
2 tbsp tinned sweetcorn kernels, drained
1 spring onion
1 tbsp groundnut oil
1 garlic clove, peeled and crushed
½ tsp ground cumin
½ tsp paprika
A pinch of turmeric
100g paella rice
330ml vegetable stock, made using a low-salt stock cube
A little ground black pepper (optional)

The first and most important job is to prepare all the vegetables, be that cutting, snipping, weighing or tasting; let the kids get as involved as you dare. Deseed and chop the red pepper, quarter the tomatoes, measure the peas and sweetcorn and slice the spring onion into rounds. Usually as the last vegetable is being prepared they get a little bored and wander off. This is your cue to begin the less child-friendly frying part.

Gently heat the oil in a large frying pan. Add the garlic, spices and rice and fry for 1 minute, stirring constantly. Add the red pepper, tomatoes and stock and bring to the boil. Reduce the heat and let gently simmer for 10–15 minutes, uncovered, without stirring.

Towards the end of the cooking, add the peas and sweetcorn. When the rice is cooked through (try it for bite – if your child will only eat it very soft then you may need to add a little more water) remove from the heat and set aside to cool for 5 minutes. Divide between bowls, sprinkle with the spring onions and a little black pepper and serve.

Homemade rice cake dipped fish fingers

This is a production-line dinner for when you're feeling pretty tired. Yes, there will be more mess than if you made them yourself but the children are far more likely to clean their plates having had a hand in the making. And there's lots of dipping and crushing resulting in smiles. And when I'm tired little things like that make me feel less so.

Makes 8

1 white fish fillet (about 180g)
1 or 2 x 22g packs rice cakes
    (cheese flavour work well)
2 tbsp plain flour
A pinch of ground black pepper
    (optional)
1 large egg
A pinch of salt

Here there are lots of little jobs to keep everyone busy. One person needs to cut the fish into finger-shaped strips – I use scissors for ease. One person needs to crush the rice cakes up by placing them in a sealed food bag and using a rolling pin to smash them. One person needs to season the flour with black pepper and mix. And someone needs to crack the egg, add the salt and beat it.

Preheat the oven to 190°C/gas mark 5. Set up the production line. Line up, in order, a plate of fish, a plate of flour, a plate of egg, a plate of crushed up rice cakes and a baking tray lined with greaseproof paper. Then each child can take it in turns to dip the fish into the flour, then egg, then rice cakes and place spaced out on the baking tray. Bake for 10 minutes and serve with tartare sauce, mayonnaise, tomato ketchup or simply as is. These taste great in a bun or with a side of faux chips (page 44).

Mexicana bubblegum bread

I met my friend Jasmine when we were sweet 16, studying A Level philosophy. I found philosophy a tough subject; the lessons were slightly wasted on my teenage self. I no longer read Descartes but I do still love to hang out with Jasmine. She is now a PhD student in San Francisco, with her Yankee husband and baby daughter. I made this with my eldest son the last time she came for the summer to remind her of the Mexican bakeries back in her adopted home town. Her daughter loved them in pink but you can make them any colour you like, and you can even try marbling two colours together.

Makes 81 tiny rolls

500g strong white flour,
   plus extra for dusting
7g fast action dried yeast
5g salt
15ml olive oil, plus extra
   for shaping
Gel food colouring
300ml warm water

Mix together the flour, yeast, salt and oil. Add a dab of food colouring to the water. You can add as much or as little as you like. I added a fingernail amount of pink gel colouring and let Charlie stir it up. Add the water to the flour mixture then either knead by hand for about 8 minutes (see page 133) or knead in a stand mixer with a dough hook for 4 minutes on a low speed until smooth and elastic looking. Pop into a bowl and cover with cling film. Leave to double in size; the time is dependent on the room – the cooler the room, the longer it will take. Wash yours and any helper's hands straight away as the gel colours can have staying power.

Once risen, deflate the dough by knocking it back. Use scissors to divide it up into pieces about the size of a cherry tomato. Roll each piece between the palm of your hands (oil your hands if you find that the dough is sticking) and then place on a floured baking tray in a grid fashion, about 1cm apart. Cover loosely with cling film and leave to double in size again; they will spread into each other as they prove.

Preheat the oven to 220°C/gas mark 7 and bake for about 10–15 minutes until the rolls are lightly browned and well risen. Leave to cool on a wire rack. Enjoy dipped in soup, sandwiched with chocolate spread or just split and filled with cheese for a very exciting lunch indeed.

Popcorn & white chocolate all-American chewy cookies

The last time I made these they didn't work. Wait! It wasn't the recipe's fault. It was the oven. The element had blown and when I retrieved them, they were raw. I scraped them back into the bowl, slammed it in the fridge and called a friend. Armed with baking trays, raw cookie dough and a bottle of thank-you fizz, I marched round in a huff. The resulting cookies were perfect. All inner chew, outer crunch and they'd barely spread. You see, the chilled dough made for perfectly shaped cookies. A happy accident.

Makes about 34

- 285g self-raising flour
- ½ tsp baking powder
- 170g salted butter
- 220g soft dark brown sugar
- 100g caster sugar
- 1 large egg plus 1 large egg yolk, at room temperature
- 1 tbsp vanilla extract
- 100g white chocolate chips
- 30g sweet popcorn, broken up into halves and quarters

Mix together the flour and baking powder until evenly combined. Place the butter in a microwaveable bowl and melt in the microwave for about 1 minute. Set aside and leave to cool until you can dip a finger into it. In another bowl and using a wooden spoon, mix together the melted butter and both sugars until well combined. Add the whole egg and yolk and the vanilla extract and beat again. Add the flour and baking powder to the wet mixture and beat until you can't see any trace of the flour. Lastly stir in the white chocolate chips and the popcorn pieces. Chill the dough in the fridge for 30 minutes.

Preheat the oven to 160°C/gas mark 3. Line 4 baking trays with non-stick greaseproof paper. Roll small pieces of the mixture into plum-sized balls (about 25g) and squash flat until about 1cm high. Place on the baking sheets with gaps of 4cm between each to allow them to spread during baking. Bake in batches in the centre and top of the oven for about 10 minutes until the sides are starting to brown but the middles are soft looking and puffed up. Remove from the oven and allow to cool on the trays. Serve with tall glasses of ice-cold milk.

Award-winning Chocolate Tiffin

This is up there with being one of my major life achievements. Yes, having babies and getting married and passing exams are all hugely important in the grand scheme of things. But a *Blue Peter* badge? Now that's something I'll bore on about forever. And here's the recipe that won it. Beware: this is sickly sweet. I've suggested cutting it into 25 small squares but you may want to go smaller. Substitute the biscuits as you wish.

Makes about 25 small squares

50g butter, plus extra
   for greasing
350g milk chocolate,
   broken into pieces
150g oat biscuits or digestives
   (about 10 biscuits)
50g dried apricots, chopped
50g raisins
70g glacé cherries, halved
3 nougat and caramel
   chocolate bars, refrigerated
   and sliced (I use Mars Bars)

Grease and line a 20 x 20cm baking tin with non-stick greaseproof paper. Place the butter and chocolate in a microwaveable bowl and melt in the microwave for short bursts (this should take about 1 minute) or place the bowl over a pan of simmering water, ensuring the bottom of the bowl does not come into contact with the water. Stir until completely melted and smooth and set aside to cool a little.

Place the biscuits in a sealed food bag and bash them with a rolling pin into 2cm pieces. Tip the broken biscuits, dried fruit and glacé cherries into the melted chocolate mixture and stir well. Add the chocolate bar pieces and stir again until well mixed through. Spoon the mixture into the prepared tin and cover with a piece of cling film. Press down to achieve a flat-ish top then chill for 2 hours before cutting into squares and eating in front of Blue Peter.

What I want and what my children want are very different things. I dream of a sun lounger, the chance to read a book cover to cover and an icy G&T served pool side with a nosebag chaser of salted nibbles. Conversely, my children dream of trains, trampolines and treasure to hunt.

When it comes to their birthdays I make a point of trying to remember back to what it was like to be a child. To worry about who sat next to you when the jelly was served, whether the music would stop when the parcel was passed across your lap and whether Mummy had remembered to put a balloon and bubbles in the party bags. Important and troubling stuff when you're five.

These ideas have all been well received by my sons and their friends but don't go mad and make them all. I'd choose two sweet, two savoury and something to house the candles for the Happy Birthday sing-along. If you can, add to that lots of mums and dads to hoover up the leftovers as kids always eat less at parties than we grown-ups think. They're too busy being statues, pinning tails or passing parcels. We could learn a thing or two from them.

Children's Party Food

(Because You're Only Old Once)

Pizza parties

I find a foodie activity gives the party some focus, helps with the catering and pleases lots of different palates. I make the dough ahead, divide it into portions, freeze it in bags and defrost at room temperature the morning of the party. You can also freeze the tomato sauce in ice-cube trays and just defrost when needed. Each child gets their own dough, a small rolling pin and access to a myriad of toppings. Worry not about space in the oven if your child has a lot of pals. Just bake and serve cold. They still taste great.

Makes about 20 tiny pizzas, 12 small ones or 7 large

For the pizza base:

650g strong white flour

7g fast action dried yeast

2 tsp salt

50ml buttermilk (or use milk with a bit of lemon juice)

30ml olive oil

325ml warm water

A little semolina, for dusting

For the topping:

400g tin of chopped tomatoes

2 tbsp tomato purée

2 tbsp olive oil

1 tsp dried oregano

1 tsp salt

1 tbsp sugar

Mozzarella, thinly sliced

Any other toppings you fancy

Ideas for buttermilk

For a quick soda bread, mix 500g plain flour with 10g bicarbonate of soda, 1 teaspoon of salt and a pinch of dried oregano, bind with buttermilk and make up to 400g using natural yoghurt; shape and bake at 200°C/gas mark 6 for 40 minutes.

To make the dough mix together the flour, yeast and salt in a bowl, then add the buttermilk, oil and water. Knead by hand for 8 minutes or in a stand mixer with a dough hook for 4 minutes on a low speed until smooth and elastic. Cover in cling film (or a clean shower cap!) and leave to double in size. The cooler the room, the slower the rise. Perversely, the longer the rise the better the flavour, so if you have time, prove in a cool place.

Simmer the tomatoes, purée, oil, oregano, salt and sugar over a low heat for 30 minutes, until the sauce is thick and rich.

Once the dough has risen, deflate it by punching it down or giving it a few turns with the dough hook. Portion up and freeze if not using now.

When ready to cook, preheat the oven to the hottest it will go, at least 200°C/gas mark 6, and place the shelf at the top of the oven. Dust your work surface with either semolina or flour. Take a ball of your slightly sticky pizza dough (I use 150g for an adult, 85g for a child and 50g for a toddler) and cover it all in semolina or flour. Use a rolling pin, roll the dough as thin as possible without it breaking. Don't worry about the shape.

Place the dough on a baking tray, spread a smear of tomato sauce over the top (too much makes for a soggy base) and top with mozzarella and any toppings you fancy. My eldest likes olives and tomatoes, my youngest olives and ham. Beware of overloading with wet toppings as it can make for a soggy pizza.

Bake in the oven until the edges look crisp and start to brown, about 10 minutes for mini pizzas and about 15 for larger ones. Do keep an eye on them as it all depends on how thin the dough was rolled. The thinner they are the quicker they will bake.

Baby bear claw sausage rolls your way

Sausage and indeed any pig-based food products go down very well with my children and their friends. Be it pigs in blankets, sticky honey and mustard chipolatas, or the great sausage roll, they love them all. These are especially well received as they involve fashioning pork and buttery puff pastry into baby bear claws.

Makes 16 claws

Plain flour, for dusting
500g pack of chilled puff pastry
8 good-quality chipolatas
Extra filling ideas: wholegrain mustard, sweet chilli sauce, caramelised onions, grated cheese, dried cranberries, finely chopped dried apricots, grated apple, chopped cooked bacon, finely chopped chives
A pinch of salt
1 egg

Preheat the oven to 220°C/gas mark 7 and line 2 baking trays with non-stick greaseproof paper. On a lightly floured surface, roll the pastry out to about the thickness of a pound coin and to a 45 x 20cm rectangle. Cut the pastry in half lengthways so that you have two thin strips measuring 45 x 10cm. Take 4 sausages, cut a hole in the end of the casings and push the meat out directly onto the centre of one of the pastry strips. Continue until the whole strip of pastry has a line of sausage down the middle, leaving a 2cm gap from each edge. Repeat for the other strip of pastry with the remaining chipolatas.

Add whatever extra fillings you think your crowd will like. Grated apple goes down very well with younger ones and wholegrain mustard and bacon with the older. Add the salt to the egg and beat well. Paint the egg wash down one long edge of each piece of pastry and fold the opposite long edge over to meet it, pressing down to seal. Cut the pastry into 5cm pieces, making 8 sausage rolls from each strip. Place the rolls on the baking trays, then use scissors to snip four 1cm-deep cuts into the sealed pastry edges to make the 'claws' on each one. Egg wash over all of the rolls completely. When all the rolls are ready, bake for 20 minutes until well risen, golden and cooked through. Serve warm or cold to baby bears.

Cheese & onion straws

It's a pity children don't come with an instruction manual. I'd like to know how to deal with the tantrums that ensue after helping to open a drink I've been asked to. Or how to console a two-year-old incandescent with rage at being unable to climb a slide without slipping down it. If I had any input into the instruction manual it would have these cheese and onion straws originally devised by Anuszka's mum, for they produce toothy grins and rounded chipmunk cheeks; the holy grail of parenting.

Makes 26

175g plain flour, plus extra for dusting
2 tsp mustard powder
20g onion sprinkles, crispies or ready to eat fried onions
100g salted butter, cut into 1cm cubes
100g Parmesan, grated
1 large egg, beaten

Mix together the flour, mustard powder and onion sprinkles until well combined. Use clean hands to rub in the butter until you have a fine breadcrumb-like consistency, then stir in the cheese. Add the beaten egg and use a blunt knife to mix and pull the mixture together. Wrap in cling film and chill for 10 minutes.

Preheat the oven to 200°C/gas mark 6 and line 2 baking trays with non-stick greaseproof paper. Roll out the pastry to a 1cm thickness on a lightly floured work surface. Cut into straws, each about 1.5 x 10cm, place on the baking trays and bake for 10–15 minutes until browned and baked through. Remove from the tray and leave to cool on a wire rack and serve as a cheesy alternative to crisps.

Ideas for onion sprinkles

Dip chicken strips in flour, beaten egg and then breadcrumbs mixed with onion sprinkles before baking for 20 minutes at 180°C/gas mark 4 to make low-fat chicken dippers. Or use to top shepherd's pie. Or make yeasted bread swirls following the St Clements recipe on page 136, but using butter and onion sprinkles as the filling rather than sugar and zest, then painting with egg wash before baking for a shiny glaze.

Rocky road Florentines

The crunch and all-important brushing of chocolate make Florentines a big hit amongst the smaller people in our family. Add to this already heady combination some marshmallows and sultanas and this could well be treat heaven. Obviously exercise caution should any of your children's friends have a nut allergy.

Makes 14

115g honey
100g brown granulated sugar
45g plain flour
200g flaked almonds
170g good-quality milk
    chocolate
100g glacé cherries, cut into
    halves with scissors
30g mini marshmallows
20g rich tea biscuits (about
    2 biscuits), chopped into
    1cm pieces
30g sultanas

Preheat the oven to 190°C/gas mark 5 and line 2 baking trays with non-stick greaseproof paper. Heat the honey and sugar in a saucepan over a medium heat until the mixture is molten and the sugar has nearly completely dissolved. Remove from the heat and stir in the flour and almonds using a wooden spoon. Leave to cool for 2–3 minutes and then place heaped tablespoons onto the baking sheets about 3cm apart, to allow for a little spreading. Do not use your fingers to get the mixture off the spoon as it will be extremely hot. Squash them down a little with the back of a spoon as you do not want heaped mounds. Bake for 10 minutes until lovely, golden and they have spread. Remove from the oven and leave to cool on the trays.

Melt the chocolate in a heatproof bowl over a saucepan of barely simmering water, making sure that the base of the bowl does not touch the water. Stir until completely melted. Spoon a couple of teaspoons of chocolate onto the top of each Florentine and press a few cherries, marshmallows, biscuit pieces and sultanas into it. Repeat for each one and if there's any chocolate leftover, drizzle it over the top of the Florentines in a zigzag pattern. Leave the chocolate to set for 2 hours.

Ideas for glacé cherries

Dip in melted dark chocolate and leave to dry on greaseproof paper, then package up for an easy present. Or make the chocolate cake on page 202, and fill and cover with whipped cream laced with cherry brandy, then top with glacé cherries and grated chocolate for a cheat's Black Forest gâteau.
Or you can just add them to cupcakes or a tiffin.

Chocolate orange rice crispy cakes

As I age it's the little stuff that makes me happy. At 25 all I wanted was the wind through my hair as I drove a sporty soft-top car. Now, I am far happier with the wind through my hair as I bounce with my boys on a trampoline or run down the hill at our local park. Similarly, complicated restaurant food is rare and lovely, but given the choice I'm more likely to choose something simple. And it doesn't get easier than this.

Makes 12

275g good-quality milk chocolate, finely chopped
1 tsp good-quality orange extract
110g rice crispies
110g chocolate orange balls (I use Aero) or other orange coloured or flavoured sweets that you fancy

Line a 12-hole cupcake tin with cases. Place the chocolate and orange extract in a large, dry microwaveable bowl (water is not a friend of chocolate). Heat in the microwave until melted, about 1 minute, or placed over a pan of simmering water, being careful not to let the water come into contact with the bottom of the bowl. Stir gently until the chocolate has completely melted then add the rice crispies and stir again until they're all well coated.

Spoon the mixture into the cupcake cases and press a few sweets onto the top. Leave the cakes to set for a couple of hours before serving.

Cupcake decorating parties

Either decorate these the day before, or let them decorate their own. If leaving them to it, make one or two for them to copy. Factor in plenty of hands-on time for a couple of adults to help. The almonds give the cakes a longer shelf life so they can be made up to three days in advance and kept un-iced in tins. If iced, don't keep in the fridge or an airtight container as the fondant will sweat. Instead, cover loosely with cling film.

Makes 15 cupcakes

For the animal toppers:

Sugarpaste in every colour you can think of. Allow 250g per child as a lot gets eaten/ relegated to the floor. If you are decorating them yourself you need barely 65g per cake for the animal toppers (250g per princess though)

Icing sugar, for dusting

For the cakes:

100g self-raising flour
150g caster sugar
150g butter or margarine, softened
50g ground almonds (or substitute with more flour)
1 tsp baking powder
1 tbsp vanilla extract
3 large eggs, at room temperature

For the buttercream:

120g butter
240g icing sugar
2 tbsp vanilla extract
Gel food colouring (optional)

The day before making your decorations, use a rolling pin to roll the sugarpaste out onto a surface that has been very lightly dusted with icing sugar (if you use too much the sugarpaste will dry up), to a thickness of about ¾cm. Cut out circles using a cutter, then leave to dry until hard on non-stick greaseproof paper overnight. This will act as a stand.

Preheat the oven to 170°C/gas mark 3 and line a 12-hole cupcake tin with cases. Beat all the cake ingredients with an electric mixer for 4 minutes or with a wooden spoon for 8 minutes, until light and creamy. Spoon a heaped tablespoon of the batter into each case, until half filled. Bake for 20–25 minutes until well risen, golden and a toothpick comes out of the centre clean. Leave to cool on a wire rack.

Make the buttercream. Beat the butter until soft and creamy, then add 1 tablespoon of icing sugar at a time and beat well after each addition. Once all the sugar has been added, mix in the vanilla and beat for 7 minutes with a mixer or about 10 minutes with a wooden spoon to ensure the icing is really light and airy. Add food colouring if you like at this stage.

Spoon a tablespoon of buttercream onto the cooled cake and top with a sugarpaste stand. Fashion any animals that you fancy from the sugarpaste, using water to attach limbs to the body and stand. Use a well-washed garlic press to make grass and a toothpick to indent eyes. You can buy cutters but they are not necessary; everything in the photograph was made by hand.

To make a princess, unpeel the cake from the case, turn the cake upside down, cover it in buttercream and drape with a sugarpaste dress. Add a head, body, arms, a bolero to hide any joins and a cone-shaped hat studded with sprinkle jewels.

Strawberry milkshake honey butterflies

My life is not pink. Not in any way. It is full of spiders and snails and stones and sticks. For I am the mother of boys, and I am truly happy with my lot. However, I recently became Godmother to a little girl so I now get to indulge my girlie side through her. These are the biscuits I will be making for her first birthday. If pink isn't the favourite colour then banana milkshake powder works equally well.

Makes about 10 fully fledged butterflies

For the biscuits:

75g butter
75g soft light brown sugar
30ml honey
225g plain flour, plus extra
    for dusting
1 tbsp water

For the icing:

65g butter
185g icing sugar
25g strawberry
    milkshake powder
Sugar sprinkles

Melt the butter, sugar and honey in a pan over a very low heat until dissolved. Use a wooden spoon to stir in the flour until you have a very stiff dough, adding water to pull it together. Add a tiny bit more if it is still crumbly, but the less water the better. Wrap in cling film and chill for 30 minutes.

Make the icing. Beat the butter in a bowl until soft then add the icing sugar and milkshake powder a tablespoon at a time, mixing after each addition. You want a very stiff icing so don't beat until it is light and fluffy; it should be mouldable not pipeable. If it won't come together, scrunch it up with your hands.

Preheat the oven to 170°C/gas mark 3 and line 2 baking trays with non-stick greaseproof paper. On a lightly floured surface, roll the dough out to a 5mm thickness. Don't worry if it cracks, just squash it back together. Cut out twenty 6cm diameter circles and cut 10 of them in half to make wings. Place the circles and semi-circles on the trays about 2cm apart in case they spread during baking. Bake in the oven for 10–15 minutes until just starting to brown. Leave to cool completely on a wire rack.

Assemble the biscuits using 25g of icing per butterfly. Use some icing to make 2 thin sausages to attach to the straight edges of a pair of wings, then squash into a plate filled with sprinkles. Use the remainder of the icing to form two balls and squash these onto the middle of the circular biscuit base, leaving a 5mm gap. Balance the wings in the middle of the balls, so that the decorated edges are facing out. Squash down gently and repeat with the remaining icing and biscuits. Leave to dry until the revellers descend.

Over the rainbow meringues

Is there anything more joyful in appearance than a mountainous, brilliant white meringue? The whitest caster sugar and fresh, cold egg whites make for the best, most impressive snowy-peaked meringues. The colourful swirls can of course be themed to the party boy or girl's favourite colour.

Makes 9 tiny meringues, scale up as required

1 large egg (older eggs are slightly better)
A pinch of cream of tartar
60g caster sugar
Gel food colouring

Preheat the oven to 90°C/gas mark ¼ or its lowest setting. The hotter the oven the more the meringues will be an off-white. Line 2 baking trays with foil, shiny side up.

Separate your egg. I use the shell – pass the yolk from half shell to half shell until all the white has dropped into a bowl below. Or hold the entire egg in a splayed hand, letting the white fall through your fingertips whilst holding on to the yolk. Or you can use an egg separator contraption. Keep the yolk for another use.

Whisk the white and cream of tartar in a large bowl until soft peaks form, about 3 minutes with a mixer and 5–7 by hand. Add the sugar 1 tablespoon at a time, whisking after each addition. Don't chuck the lot in and hope for the best as you'll end up with meringues with sugary strands. When all the sugar has been absorbed they'll be a glossy, brilliant white and stand up to very stiff peaks. Dip a teaspoon into the colouring and swirl in the meringue for a ripple effect. Use a maximum of 2 colours to avoid hues sludging together.

Heap tablespoons onto the trays, spaced 4cm apart to allow for swelling. Bake for 40 minutes before testing; they're ready when they easily come away from the foil but are not coloured. This can take up to 2 hours. Turn the oven off and leave to cool in the oven if possible (this prevents the cracking that occurs from a sudden change in temperature) or on a wire rack if not.

Ideas for egg yolks

Pop the spare yolk(s) into an ice-cube tray and freeze, then transfer to a freezer bag and thaw as required in the fridge overnight. Or use to make lime or lemon curd (see page 34).

Squidgy spider's web cakes

I love the novelty of these and the ease with which they are achieved. Who knew that dragging a toothpick through icing could produce such a thing of beauty? Kids love these for obvious bug-related reasons. Adults love them for their squelchy chocolate hit. I don't use expensive chocolate, just mid-range stuff. And they're so dense, fudgy and filling that kids are happy with just the one. Meaning less batch baking for you.

Makes 12 cupcakes

For the cakes:

50g white chocolate
50g milk chocolate
50g dark chocolate
100g plain flour
100g dark brown sugar
3 tbsp cocoa powder
¾ tsp baking powder
75ml sunflower oil
50ml double cream
50ml cold water
1 large egg, at room
    temperature

For the ganache:

250g white chocolate
125ml double cream
Chocolate or black writing
    icing tube (found in the
    baking aisle)

Preheat the oven to 180°C/gas mark 4 and place the shelf in the middle of the oven. Fill a 12-hole cupcake tin with cases. Break all the chocolate up into pieces and place in a food processor with the blade attachment fitted. Whizz until you have pieces the size of chocolate chips.

Put all the other cake ingredients into a bowl and use a handheld mixer to beat until smooth, about 4 minutes. Add the chocolate then spoon about a tablespoon of the mixture into the cases until just under half full, but no more than this as you will need room for the ganache. If you find you have too much mixture for your cases simply fill a few more. Bake for 20 minutes until the tops start to crack. Remove from the tin and leave to cool completely on a wire rack.

Make the ganache. Chop the chocolate finely, then gently heat the cream in a small saucepan until hot and bubbling. Remove from the heat and immediately stir through the chocolate until lovely and smooth. Pour or spoon the ganache over the cooled cakes until you have completely 'flooded' the top.

When all the cakes are covered with ganache take the icing tube and draw a spiral from the middle outwards. Immediately drag a toothpick from the centre of the cupcake to the outside 6–8 times, dragging to separate points on the top. This will create a web effect. Leave to dry completely.

'99 ice cream cakes

These indulge my love of bestowing surprises, as they look like an ice cream but hide a treasure trove of soft sponge and sweets. Transportation can be tricky as they don't stay upright easily, so I cut holes in a box and line with cake cases to hold the cones in place.

Makes 14

14 flat-bottomed ice
    cream cones
1 large egg, at room
    temperature
Caster sugar
Self-raising flour
Butter
1 tbsp vanilla extract
½ tsp baking powder
1 tbsp milk
Gel food colouring (optional)

For the buttercream:
165g salted butter, softened
325g icing sugar
2 tbsp vanilla extract

To hide and decorate:
350g sugar-coated chocolates
Small gold chocolate
    coins (optional)
14 chocolate flakes

Preheat the oven to 170°C/gas mark 3 and place your cones on a thick-bottomed, heavy baking tray. Do not use a thin tray, as these can buckle in the oven and cause the cones to topple.

Weigh the egg in its shell and note the weight. Measure out the same weight of sugar (so for an egg weighing 65g, weigh out 65g of sugar) then the same of flour and the same of butter, and place in a bowl. Add the egg, vanilla, baking powder and milk and beat until light and creamy, about 3–4 minutes with a mixer or 5–7 minutes with a wooden spoon. Add food colouring if you like. Spoon 1 heaped teaspoon of batter into each cone – this seems very little but it will rise to fill three-quarters of the cone, with room for the icing. Bake for 20–25 minutes until a toothpick comes out clean. Place on a wire rack to cool.

Make the buttercream. Beat the butter until soft and creamy, then add 1 tablespoon of icing sugar at a time, mixing well after each addition. Once all the icing sugar has been added, mix in the vanilla and beat for 7 minutes with a mixer or 10 minutes with a wooden spoon until light and airy. Attach a large star nozzle to your icing bag and rest in a pint glass, rolling the top over the rim. Spoon the mixture into the bag then hold the top and allow gravity to push the mixture to the nozzle end. Massage the bag slightly to remove any air bubbles. Stand it back in the glass.

Fill to the top of the cone with chocolates; I use about 25g per cone. Hold your icing bag upright over the cone. Using one hand to guide and the other to push the icing down the bag, pipe a swirl in one steady stream, starting at 12 o'clock and gradually moving into the middle. Start taking the pressure off your pushing hand and pull the nozzle away from the cake to finish. If you have never done this before watch a video online and practise on greaseproof paper. Or you can simply use an ice cream scoop to top with icing. Finish each with a flake.

Sticky little fingers chocolate bar cake

I think for at least a few years you can happily get away with producing a really good chocolate cake covered in yet more chocolate and maybe some sweets for a birthday party, before the obsession with shop-bought primary coloured superheroes and saccharine pink princesses takes over. The bonus with this cake is that if the children are too over-excited the mums and dads will appreciate a slice, for this is a real old-fashioned chocolate cake, the kind I remember my own mother making for celebrations. Just add candles.

Serves 10–12

For the cake:

200g salted butter, softened, plus extra for greasing
40g cocoa powder
90ml boiling water
200g caster sugar
2 tbsp vanilla extract
50g golden syrup
4 large eggs, at room temperature
200g self-raising flour

For the icing and decoration:
120g salted butter
60ml milk
60g cocoa powder
450g icing sugar
Favourite chocolate or sweets

Grease and line two 20cm cake tins and preheat the oven to 180°C/gas mark 4. In a large mixing bowl, dissolve the cocoa in the boiling water and whisk until you have a thick, smooth paste. Add all the remaining cake ingredients and beat until thick and creamy, about 4 minutes in a stand mixer, 5–6 with a hand-held electric mixer and 8 minutes with a wooden spoon.

Split the mixture equally between the two tins and bake for 25–30 minutes until a skewer comes out of the centre clean and the edges of the cakes are just starting to shrink away from the sides. Leave to cool on a wire rack for 5 minutes, or, as soon as you can bear to touch them, remove them from the tins. Be careful as they are light and fragile.

To make the icing, melt the butter and milk in a saucepan over a low heat. Sift the cocoa and icing sugar into a bowl and add 1 tablespoon of the dry mixture at a time to the wet mixture, beating well with a wooden spoon after each addition. The icing will be very thick, almost unspreadable so heat gently on the hob until it is runny enough to spread. Use half to top one cake and allow it to solidify a little before adding the second cake. Reheat the remaining icing if it has begun to set and pour it over the top. Decorate with your child's favourite sweets – my eldest loves chocolate caramel, glacé cherries and strawberries but my youngest is a purist; it's chocolate buttons all the way.

Chocolate gingerbread barn

Crazy as it may be, some children just aren't that into cake. Birthdays can be a struggle for cake-rejecters. What do you push candles into? What do you gather around to sing? I have the answer. And I think it may be just as delicious as a great big cake.

Serves 12

For the barn:
125g unsalted butter
100g dark muscovado sugar
65g golden syrup
1 tsp vanilla extract
385g plain flour
50g cocoa powder
1 tsp bicarbonate of soda
1 tsp ground cinnamon
2 tsp ground ginger
2 clear boiled sweets

Decorating and pigs:
10g cocoa powder
500g white fondant icing
1 silver ball for the door knob
2 mini marshmallows
    for the chimney
A few jelly diamonds
    to decorate around
    the windows
2 x 35g packs of chocolate
    buttons for the roof
Any other sweets you like
    the idea of – lollipops
    make great trees
Pink gel food colouring

For the mud:
150ml double cream
150g dark chocolate,
    finely chopped

Photocopy the templates on page 207 at 200%, trace them onto greaseproof paper and cut out. Preheat the oven to 200°C/gas mark 6. Melt the butter, sugar, syrup and vanilla in a pan over a low heat, not letting the mixture boil. Mix the flour, cocoa, bicarbonate of soda, cinnamon and ginger in a large bowl, then use a wooden spoon to stir in the butter mixture, making a stiff dough. Add a little water if it isn't pulling together.

Roll the warm dough on non-stick greaseproof paper to about 1–1.5cm thick. Use the templates and a sharp knife to cut 2 sides, 1 front, 1 back and 2 roof panels. Cut out the door and keep to bake. Cut the windows and discard. Re-roll any leftovers and cut into gingerbread men. The dough will harden as it cools.

Lift the paper holding the biscuits onto a baking tray; do not peel them off the paper as they will stretch. Trim the paper about 2cm wider than the biscuits. Place boiled sweets into the window holes. Bake for 12 minutes until hard. Leave to cool on the tray.

Knead the cocoa into 400g of the fondant icing until light brown and well distributed. Wrap the remaining fondant in cling film to prevent it drying out. Break off pieces of brown fondant as you need it. Roll 4 sausages of fondant and place on a tray or cake stand in the shape of the walls – use the baked pieces as a guide to help position them correctly. You want each sausage to sit so that when you place the barn walls, they'll sit in the middle of the fondant, as the fondant sausages are essentially foundations.

Use sausages of fondant to attach one side panel to the back wall, then place these on your foundations. Add another fondant sausage to the other side of the back wall and attach the other side panel, pushing it into the foundation as you work. Repeat with the front. Use the same method to add the roof, leaving a 1cm gap in the middle to house a long piece of double twisted fondant made by rolling a sausage twice the length of the roof then folding in half and twisting. If the fondant isn't sticking, brush with a little water. Let the barn dry for 30 minutes and wrap any leftover chocolate fondant in cling film.

Make the mud. Gently heat the cream in a saucepan until it starts to bubble. Take off the heat and add the chocolate, stirring until smooth. Leave in the fridge to harden, giving it an occasional stir.

Using fondant as adhesive, add a silver ball as a door handle, a marshmallow chimney, jelly diamonds as window decorations and the door. Using small pieces of the fondant brushed with water to stick, tile the roof with chocolate buttons, starting at the bottom of the panels and working upwards, slightly overlapping each row. Be careful as you work as the house will not be set.

When the mud is set to the point that it will spread but is not runny, spoon it around the house, but not too far up the sides. Use a fork to make it look messy. Massage a dot of pink food colouring into the leftover white fondant, then make pigs by attaching 4 little ball shaped feet to a larger body using water. Place the headless pig in the mud then make the head by taking a ball and sticking a small flattened disc to the front as a snout. Add two triangles as ears and use a toothpick to make eyes and nostrils. Stick the head to the body and add a twirled sausage of fondant as a curly tail. Make as many pigs as you want, though be warned that children do generally want a pig each. If you have any gingerbread men, use the remaining brown fondant to stand them upright in the mud. Leave to dry for 2 hours at room temperature before serving with candles and cheer.

TEMPLATES
ENLARGE TO 200%

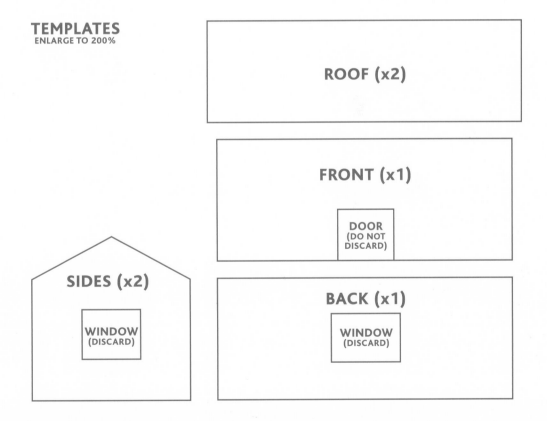

ROOF (x2)

FRONT (x1)

DOOR
(DO NOT
DISCARD)

SIDES (x2)

WINDOW
(DISCARD)

BACK (x1)

WINDOW
(DISCARD)

There is a point in life we all reach where stuff becomes less important. I realised I'd reached this landmark when my mother asked what I wanted for Christmas a few years ago. I had nothing to suggest. She insisted, as mums do, and so I asked for some new socks and T-shirts. Not exactly the thrilling gifts of my teens.

It was at about this point that I started to look at my own birthday and Christmas offerings to people a little more closely. Buying a toiletry giftset for Daddy from the boys felt pointless; the shower gel quickly forgotten, the novelty sponge falling to bits and binned by March. But a jar of gingerbread biscotti to be dipped into Christmas morning coffee leaves a memory for life. I'd rather bestow memories on people I love and care for than over packaged, easily forgotten, recycling fodder.

All the ideas in this chapter can happily be made a day or more ahead, and are usually met with a grin and a thank you. That's not to say the recipes from other chapters aren't welcome gifts. My pal Annie hand delivered a pie from 100 miles away after the birth of my first son. I can't think of anything I wanted more than dinner dealt with deliciously. Well, apart from a little sleep maybe.

Presents from the Heart

Lemon button biscuits

My nanna was a bespoke tailoress. She has tried to teach me to sew and knit over the years but I seem to have haberdasher's dyslexia. I miss stitches, misunderstand patterns, forget crucial knots and stages. Nanna was always patient, mind, as nannas should be. These days, this is as close to sewing as I get and, my, are they things of beauty. Dainty, button-shaped biscuits; zesty, pretty, rich and beautiful. Perfect little gifts.

Makes 27

225g salted butter, softened
170g caster sugar
Finely grated zest of 2 lemons
450g plain flour, plus extra
  for dusting
1 large egg

Line 3 baking sheets with non-stick greaseproof paper. Beat together the butter, sugar and lemon zest until light and creamy using an electric mixer or wooden spoon. Adding a little at a time, gently beat in the flour until well combined. Mix in the egg to bind the mixture. Wrap in cling film and chill for 1½ hours.

Roll the shortbread out on a lightly floured surface until about ¾cm thick, using a floured rolling pin. Using a 7cm cookie cutter, cut circles from the dough. Place the circles on the lined baking sheets about 2cm apart.

Then find something that is just smaller than the cutter that you used – either a smaller cutter or a glass that is about 6cm wide – and lightly press down on the centre of each button to make an indent, to represent the inner circle of the button. Do not press hard enough to cut through the dough. Use a skewer or the end of a straw to make 2 little holes in the middle of each biscuit and then chill on the baking sheets for 30 minutes.

Preheat the oven to 180°C/gas mark 4. Bake the biscuits for 10–12 minutes in the middle of the oven until just starting to brown at the edges. Remove the buttons from the trays and leave to cool on a wire rack. Place a few in a gift bag and tie with a pretty ribbon, or thread some thin ribbon through the holes if you're feeling extra genteel.

Chocolate rum and raisin fudge

Is rum and raisin too retro a flavour? I remember as a kid sneaking a lick of my mum's rum and raisin ice cream on holiday in Cornwall and feeling terribly grown up at having ingested 'alcohol'. This recipe doesn't use real rum as it affects the setting of this type of fudge. And it does not use a sugar thermometer so it's perfect for those of us who dislike boiling sugar and who like to share their rum and raisin fudge with the kids.

Makes 16-36 squares, depending on how large you want them!

70g salted butter, cut into 1cm
    cubes, plus extra for greasing
2 tsp rum flavouring
200g marshmallows
250g milk chocolate, broken
    into pieces
140g raisins

Grease and line a 20 x 20cm baking tin with non-stick greaseproof paper. In order, place the rum flavouring, marshmallows, butter and chocolate in a saucepan. Over a low heat, gently let everything melt until completely dissolved, stirring regularly. Don't be tempted to hurry it along by turning up the heat as the chocolate will burn. It may appear grainy at one stage but continue to heat as the marshmallows will release their golden syrup and the fudge will become beautifully glossy.

When the marshmallows have melted, add the raisins, stir well and remove the pan from the heat. Immediately pour into the prepared tin – you will need to work quickly as the fudge will set on contact with cold air. Don't under any circumstances use your fingers to slide the last remnants of fudge off the spoon into the tin. It's extremely hot so please use another spoon to scrape out the last of it. Refrigerate for at least 2 hours and then cut into squares and wrap. You could gift this with a nice bottle of rum if your recipient is partial to a tipple.

Christmas red cup gingerbread biscotti

Sometimes I hate myself for being so susceptible to the sorcery of the marketing man. Gingerbread flavoured coffee in red coffee shop cups should not be something I look forward to. But I do. This is something I conjured up to accompany it. These are great to give as presents, in part because they have a two-week shelf life, so you can make them a good week ahead of Christmas.

Makes 15-20

50g blanched whole almonds
1 large egg
95g soft dark brown sugar
¼ tsp ground cinnamon
¼ tsp ground nutmeg
½ tsp ground ginger
2 cloves, ground
2 peppercorns, ground
130g plain flour
½ tsp baking powder
A pinch of salt
2 pieces of stem ginger, finely chopped (about 40g)
Sunflower oil (optional)
50g white chocolate, broken into pieces (optional)

Preheat the oven to 180°C/gas mark 4. Scatter the almonds on an ungreased baking tray and bake until just brown, around 10 minutes. Mind them, as they go from brown to burnt in seconds.

Mix the egg, sugar, cinnamon, nutmeg, ginger, cloves and peppercorns until pale, thick and creamy, about 4 minutes with an electric mixer and 7 minutes with a wooden spoon. Stir in the flour, baking powder, salt, ginger and almonds until combined.

Line a baking tray with non-stick greaseproof paper. Oil your hands if the mixture is too sticky and shape it into a 20 x 10cm rectangle on the baking tray. Bake in the oven for 20–25 minutes, until brown. Leave to cool on the tray for 5 minutes.

Transfer the log to a wooden board – be careful as it will be very hot – and use a serrated knife to cut into thin slices, about 1cm wide. Lay the slices sideways on the tray and bake for another 10–15 minutes until lovely and golden. Watch the ends as they have a tendency to burn. Remove these from the oven a little earlier if needs be and let cool on a wire rack.

If you fancy a chocolate covering for your biscotti, place the chocolate in a microwaveable bowl and melt using short bursts of the microwave, stirring each time. White chocolate is quick to burn, so alternatively you can pop the bowl over a pan of simmering water, making sure the bottom does not touch the water. Gently stir with a wooden spoon until melted.

Leave the chocolate to cool a little. Rest the biscotti on a wire rack over greaseproof paper and drizzle the chocolate over the biscotti. Leave for 2 hours to set before gift wrapping.

Double quick strawberry & rose jam

Homemade jam is one of those things I forget about. In our house, we usually make a batch because on the last day of our Suffolk holiday our foraging results in a heavy yield of what-can-we-do-with-these berries. Suddenly the urge to make jam takes over and there I am, mashing, stirring and sterilising. And then when it's all done and the toast is ready, I remember just how good homemade jam is and vow to make it more regularly. This is quick smart jam for busy bees.

Makes 2–3 jars

400g strawberries, hulled
500g jam sugar (this has added pectin)
2 tbsp rose water
15g salted butter, softened

Sterilise your jam jars. I save jars throughout the year, squirrelling them away in boxes ready for when the preserving bug hits. You can either use a dishwasher to sterilise the jars, by washing the jars and the lids on its hottest setting, or you can do it in the oven by baking the jars and lids at 180°C/gas mark 4 for at least 20 minutes. Whichever method you use just remember to fill the jars whilst they are still hot. Pouring hot jam into cold jars can result in broken glass.

Put the strawberries into a large non-aluminium saucepan and crush with the back of a fork or a potato masher. You don't want to be left with any large pieces. Pour the sugar over the fruit and add the rose water and butter. Heat gently and stir until all the sugar has dissolved. Turn up the heat so that the jam is boiling so vigorously that you can't stir the bubbles away with a wooden spoon. Boil like this for 4 minutes then remove from the heat and carefully spoon into the still warm sterilised jars. Immediately screw the lid on to form a seal. This way, if the jar, lid and jam are all hot then a waxed disc isn't necessary – though if you prefer to use them you'll find them in the baking aisle.

Once cool make sure to write the name on a sticky label, otherwise you may clean forget what jam this is!

Dukkah

At a wonderful wedding of two dear friends each guest received a tiny bottle of olive oil and a packet of homemade dukkah, an Egyptian dry dip. My love affair with this spicy toasted dip was born. This stuff is moreish. Let's not just restrict this to wedding favours, use it as a starter or adapt it to make your own family blend. Dried coconut, cinnamon and almonds are great additions. And don't just scoop it up with olive oil soaked flatbreads – sprinkle over pasta bakes, grilled meats and even serve with a cheese board for a lazy, interesting finish to any meal.

Makes about 265g, enough for 8 small bags

100g sesame seeds
100g blanched hazelnuts, finely chopped
50g coriander seeds
10g cumin seeds
10g sea salt
5g ground black pepper
5g caster sugar
A generous pinch of dried mint
A pinch of dried chilli flakes

Take a frying pan and put it on the hob over a low heat. Place a large, dry bowl next to the hob – this is where you're going to tip the toasted dukkah components in batches.

Toast the sesame seeds gently in the dry frying pan until just starting to colour and they start to smell divine. Immediately tip the lot into the clean dry bowl. Add the hazelnuts to the pan and again cook until they are beginning to colour, then add to the bowl. Nuts and seeds can toast in seconds so don't take your eye off the pan. Toast the coriander seeds for a few seconds, add to the bowl and then toast the cumin seeds, tipping them into the bowl. Leave them all to cool.

Lastly add the salt, black pepper, sugar, dried mint and chilli flakes to the bowl of toasted nuts and seeds. Grind it all in a pestle and mortar or blitz very briefly in a food processor until it looks breadcrumb-like in consistency. Too much processing can result in a paste so a gentle touch is needed. Bag up and spread the dukkah love. This will happily keep for 1 month.

Lady Grey's Gin

I am friends with a Lady. She's not an actual lady, just nick-named that for her impeccable manners. Lady V, as I call her, adores a cup of Lady Grey tea. This infused gin results in a Lady's G&T that is fragrant, flowery and citrusy all at the same time.

Makes 350ml, fills 2 small bottles

35cl gin
2 Lady Grey teabags

Pour the gin into a clean bowl and add the teabags. Stir well and leave for 2 hours. Strain, bottle and write a little label with instructions to serve on the terrace with full fat tonic and a flamed twist each of lemon and orange over plenty of ice.

Bell blend garam masala

Being a girl from Leicester, curry is almost part of my DNA. I remember my first 'proper' curry at the age of six and it was quite simply the beginning of a sensory love affair. Garam masala is a blend of spices; in India the composition differs according to region. Here's my Leicestershire Bell blend but meddle away and produce your own.

Fry the ingredients one by one in a dry frying pan over a medium heat – and open the windows and doors if the weather allows as the aroma can be a little overpowering in an airless setting. Start with the coriander seeds; once they're a light brown colour tip them into a bowl away from the heat. Next toast the cumin seeds; once they start to colour add them to the bowl. Fry the peppercorns, cloves and cardamom pods together and once you see the pods start to lose their green colour add them to the bowl. Fry the fennel seeds and once you see them start to darken add them to the bowl. Lastly fry the ground cinnamon and bay leaves until they start to smell aromatic, then tip these into the pan. Leave to cool.

After 30 minutes the spices should be completely cool. Grind them all to a fine powder using a pestle and mortar or a mini food processor. Bag up the mixture with a cinnamon stick in each bag and use within 3 months.

Makes about 65g

45g coriander seeds
10g cumin seeds
5g black peppercorns
3 cloves
3 green cardamom pods
5g fennel seeds
2 tsp ground cinnamon
2 dried bay leaves
2 cinnamon sticks

Warm-your-cockles ginger vodka

Warming, with a little kick at the back of the throat, this is delicious drunk straight from the freezer as an aperitif or in a winter cocktail. Before you start, you'll need to find a jar large enough to hold your bottle of vodka as well as the fresh ginger. I use a clean preserving jar. Or you could remove a few shots from the bottle and stuff the ginger through the neck. A word on the vodka: the main flavour here will be the warming ginger so let's not get too precious about buying triple distilled vodka, though if that's what's sitting in your cupboard, then so be it.

Makes 350ml

35cl vodka
6cm piece of fresh ginger

Firstly, if you're using a preserving jar, make sure it is as clean as can be. A good scrub with some good washing up liquid and a rinse with scalding hot water should do the trick. Leave to dry naturally, then pour your vodka into it.

Chop the ginger into slices about 2–3mm thick, leaving the skin on (the skin holds lots of oil and flavour so it helps to make a more fragrant vodka). Drop the ginger into the jar/bottle of vodka. Seal and leave in a dark place for a month, giving it a little swirl every other day. I leave mine in the pantry near the cereals as I know I'll remember the daily shaking ritual that way.

After a week, taste to test the level of heat and whether you like it. If it's just right then strain the vodka through a sieve into another container, discard the ginger and bottle the vodka. If you fancy a bit more of a kick then just leave it for another week.

Don't forget to include a couple of cocktail ideas with the present. From a simple boozy ginger ale (1 shot of ginger vodka topped up with ginger ale and ice), to my Honey Bee Kicker (1 shot of ginger vodka, a tablespoon of lemon juice and a tablespoon of runny honey, shaken up and topped with dry cider).

Raspberry vinegar olives

Every Christmas we get a hamper from our friends. A bottle of raspberry vinegar appeared one year and at a loss as to what to do with it, I poured it into a half empty jar of olives. What a result… a happy marinating accident. You can buy raspberry vinegar but the flavour will be better if you make your own. You know how busy you are.

Makes 3 jars

100g raspberries,
    fresh or frozen
280ml white wine vinegar
30g caster sugar
3 x 350g jars of pitted black
    olives (each 165g drained)
About 215ml extra virgin
    olive oil

Discard any raspberries that are past their best. Place in a bowl and pour over the vinegar. Stir, mash with a fork, cover with cling film and refrigerate for 5 days.

Pass the raspberries through a fine sieve, letting the vinegar drip into a small non-aluminium saucepan. Either throw the raspberries away or use to marinate pork chops. Add the sugar to the vinegar and heat until boiling. Quickly turn down the heat so it's barely simmering. Don't continue to boil whatever you do. After 10 minutes, remove the pan from the heat and leave to cool. You should have about 235ml of vinegar.

Drain the brine from the olives. Add a third of the raspberry vinegar to each jar and then top up with olive oil until all the olives are covered and the liquid is almost to the top. Screw the lids back on and give them a shake. Pop a little label on them saying not to eat for at least a month to let the flavours develop. Store in the fridge (the oil will solidify – worry not) though allow the olives to come to room temperature before eating for optimum flavour.

INDEX

Acknowledgements

Written, stirred and baked to the sound of: The Rolling Stones, Arcade Fire, Sufjan Stevens, Tom Odell, Mr. Scruff and a dodgy Buddha Bar CD brought back from Thailand in 1999.

Thanks to:

Friends, family and other animals.

To all the vocal readers of www.recipesfromanormalmum.com; the silent readers, the Facebook page likers and the twitter followers, quite simply, thanks for reading, making and baking. You have no idea how happy you make me.

My mum and dad for their never-ending support, endless baby-sitting at incredibly short notice and general selflessness. I am indeed a spoilt only child and I love it.

My husband, what an amazing man; not only does he go out and bring home the bacon, he also cooks, he cleans, he sews, he does night feeds and he even tests recipes. My one true love.

My sons Charlie and Max, for being the best little guinea pigs a mummy can have. Mothering you has made me such a bigger and better person in so many ways. I love you.

Anuszka Stepien-Hales for her tea and sympathy, her kitchen and her mum's cheese straw recipe. You're a superstar friend for life with a fabulous name.

All the pals who have been there over the last few years, listening and coaching and being generally lovely: Georgie, Sandya, Eva, Alison and last but not least Caitlin for propping me up with her hippy, motivational daily messages and literal lending.

A special mention to Jo for always keeping the faith.

The person who wishes to remain nameless for their buckets of technical support.

Wanda Hex, Mark Willock and Deborah Stepien for kind permission to print their wonderful recipes.

The professionals.

The wonderful team at Quadrille. To Jane O'Shea for saying yes. To Helen and Arielle for making this book a thing of beauty, and especially to Arielle for her never-ending Antipodean sunny optimism and laughter. To Louise for her patience with my spelling, punctuation and grammar.

To David Loftus, for making everything in your wake beautiful. So very clever.

My literary agent Ariella Feiner for finding me, believing in me and making me endlessly re-write to achieve the best I can. I cannot thank you enough for all your hard work, patience and kindness.

My other agent (how greedy!) Graeme Legg, for all your hard work, your humour and for repeating Aesop's fables to me. You were right and you're a tonic. I wish I could bottle you.

The ever supportive folk at Sainsbury's, KitchenAid, QVC and Seven.

Love Productions, for picking me to take part in the ride of a lifetime.